P9-DUB-556

CLARENCE MAJOR

Painted Turtle:
Woman with Guitar

SUN &
MOON

CLASSICS

73

LOS ANGELES
SUN & MOON PRESS
1996

Sun & Moon Press
A Program of The Contemporary Arts Educational Projects Inc.
a nonprofit corporation
6026 Wilshire Boulevard, Los Angeles, California 90036

This edition first published in paperback in 1996 by Sun & Moon Press
10 9 8 7 6 5 4 3 2
FIRST PAPERBACK EDITION
©1988 by Clarence Major
Biographical material ©1996 by Sun & Moon Press

This book was made possible, in part, through an operational grant from
the Andrew W. Mellon Foundation, through a matching grant from
the National Endowment for the Arts, and through contributions to
The Contemporary Arts Educational Project, Inc.,
a nonprofit corporation

The author wishes to thank the Fellowship Council on
Research and Creative Work of the Graduate School at the
University of Boulder for a grant which made this book possible.

Cover: *Wall Hanging,* Nellie Nelson (Lukachukai, Arizona)
Design: Katie Messborn

LIBRARY OF CONGRESS CATALOGING IN PUBLICATION DATA
Major, Clarence [1936]
Painted Turtle: Woman with Guitar
p. cm—(Sun & Moon Classics: 73)
ISBN: 1-55713-085-X
I. Title. II. Series.
811´.54—dc20

Printed in the United States of America on acid-free paper.

Painted Turtle:
Woman with Guitar

Prologue

I nkpen sent me to her to make her more commercial, to get her to switch to electric. I never liked the idea all the way but I wasn't sure it wouldn't be good for her to rake in a little more money and to get off the grimy cantina circuit. I liked her music on the demos he played for me.

If she was telling her own story she'd start it with *Sonahchi*. She was that culturally bound. That seriousness and lack of ambiguity were part of her charm. Did I say charm? I never met a charming southwestern Indian in my life! Even us Navajos (and I'm part Hopi) never went in for good old American charm. They'll tell you my father's people, the Navajos, were like the rest of them, part of nature, but don't believe it.

I kicked around a lot before I decided to try music. That summer when I picked up a guitar, it happened to be electric. It happened one night in a cantina in Sante Fe. This Mexican group let me sit in with them. They said I was a natural. But even then I knew it wasn't me, that the real me was somewhere else, in a quieter place.

She was on when I went in. A drunk at the bar was talking baseball real loud, arguing scores with the bartender. This was the first time I heard her sing her "Twins of the Sun." That one-string-at-a-time guitar kept leaping between her words like tongue-flames between the toes of a firewalker. I sat quietly in a corner and watched. She went next into another one I had heard on the demo, "Call Me Makki." She didn't bother to tell the audience what makki meant and I liked that. She held her guitar right and the tilt of her chin was just right for the light and her buckskin gave her the right kind of warm contrast to her skin which was only slightly lighter than the buckskin. I watched her eyes. She never once looked in my direction.

When she finished I took my guitar with me and went over to tell her how good she was—as if she needed to hear that. She smelled of mint and freshly tanned leather. Her necklace and rings and watch were of silver and turquoise and coral and mother-of-pearl and jet agate and they sparkled dimly in the dark light. This was the woman Inkpen said was making hardly enough to get from town to town on; sleeping in bus depots, in flophouses, motels at the end of the line? She gave me only a half-smile—not even that, really. Zunis are like that, especially toward us Navajos. I saw her sizing me up right away. But I didn't let that coldness stop me.

Chapter 1
Wonderment

Her father made a cradleboard while her mother was breast-feeding her. This was right after the sandbed. It became a family joke that she knocked the ear of corn off the bed. Of course she didn't. Some of the old folks later said it was the sure sign of bad luck.

She was taken off the cradleboard a month early, in the third. I've seen the old moms keep the babes on till they are a year or older. That's bad news. But that was at Tewa.

The old folks had occasion to gossip again, when the Little Turtle tried to chew the turquoise that had been placed in her cradle to keep witches and devils away.

In my mind I saw her mother as she washed the Little Turtle. When she finished she placed her in the sandbed. The mother's hands were crusty and strong and warm.

She was beginning to walk. The first step was very important. The whole family watched. As she took it near the front step, smoke from the bread-baking oven nearby swam into her face and caused her to lose her balance. She sat down in the sand and everybody laughed.

The first time she went with her mother up Corn Mountain to gather clay she was still only a toddler. Marelda used the clay to make pottery. The Little Turtle helped—or thought she helped—her mother gather the clay.

> Soaked in water
> then ground between rocks
> The hand-shaped surface
> made into a spiral
> Mudfrog handles, one
> on each side; dung-covered
> Fired in hive-shaped oven
> Olla carried to the goat-
> owner for milk

She played with the older girls in the clan. The chief of the girls and Sakisti called for her to make song. She danced as soon as she learned to walk; she danced, danced, danced, like crazy she danced; danced with the older girls in the Santu at the Sacred Plaza.

When she was bad her mother told her Atoshle would come and get her. She cried out of fear. Her father comforted her with animal stories. But the stories did not always drive away the fear. After all, Atoshle could eat a whole kid without chewing the parts. He kept the bones in his cave. He castrated little boys who played with their shuminne.

She learned early to mistrust strangers, to trust the strong odor of yucca soap, to trust its purification powers. She also learned not to wander out of the yard at night. Atoshle or some witch might grab her.

Learning was easy. She played fair in the kick race with the other girls. She avoided, even before first grade, being a bigshot. Before she was two she developed an appreciation for jewelry. She liked its sparkle; she liked the red and white brightness of her first moccasins, her first headband, her first shawl. Her father's mantas and breechcloth also attracted her eye. She liked her mother's ceremonial dress so much she put it on one day and wore it all around the house. This earned her a spanking; her first. She tried to wear her father's leggins of buckskin a week later but could find only one thong so she looked pretty silly to Marelda, so silly in fact that the act of wearing clothes not her own didn't earn her punishment this time. With her courage up, she next ventured into her father's overshoes of undressed sheepskin. She fell. She cried. She recovered. This was learning.

Learning was wonderment. The first time she saw the huge Shalako birds, feeling the excitement and fear together and the other winter dance-figures, and later the summer dancers, she changed—a little bit each time. Her spirit was altered. She lost herself in the change. But she always came back. The sounds of deer hoof-clankers rang in her ears. The smell of cottonwood in bloom and the pussywillow were, at first, stunning and stinging. She heard with surprise the gourd rattles and the sounds of the hoop dancers. In her father's arms at the lady's wood chopping contest, she shuddered from the sight of the big arms and the sound of the ax wrenching the wood apart. Seeing smoke the first few times drift up from the chimneys of the adobes was the discovery of a silent and strange presence.

Sleeping, as much as the wakeful times, was wonderment. Not only did the dancers come in the night, Atoshle could get you, anything else could happen. The night had no rules. Ghosts came from everywhere, and especially from the graves and from the lake the older people talked about.

11

Ghost dancer why
do you dance
so slowly
with such menace
while the dwellers
of the pueblo
sleep
Is the night
your sole
companion?

Chapter 2
Old Gchachu

I can just see Old Gchachu sitting at the head of the table, his only living relative, a childless daughter of fifty, sitting at the other end. I keep watching the Turtle in this setting. Maybe I watch her with the eye in the back of my head or out the corners of my real ones. Old Gchachu waves to Marelda to bring the Little Turtle over to him. The mother takes the child's hand and trots her over to the patriarch. He touches the child's head with fingers that are knotted twigs shaking in a desert storm. He tells her she will grow up to marry a priest who will be a very wise man and she will become legendary among the Zuni for her cooking of shredded lamb stew and blood pudding and hominy and sheep liver and intestines and olla podrido sauces made of chile-colorado and coriander-leaf and that she will be especially good at tchutsikwahnamuwe and legendary also for her love of children and family.

The old man calls Waldo over and Waldo stands beside Marelda and the father-of-the-clan looks at the father of the Little Turtle. Old Gchachu motions toward Marelda's pregnancy and says that the next one will be a boy who will grow up to be a greatly respected member of the Bow Priest Society.

I of course imagine this, making it up from what Painted Turtle told me. She said she was afraid of the old man. She was glad

13

when her mother led her away to help the women and the other girls again.

Being part Navajo and part Hopi myself, I can just imagine the old man Gchachu rapping his staff handle on the table top. The chatter ends. He waits till feet beneath the long scarred table stop moving. When there is only the sound of the grumbling infants and small crawling children, he says, "Everybody here now bow your head with your hands together for prayer."

Another old man whimpers, "But Larry that is the Christian way."

You can just see Old Gchachu lifting his crusted hand to stop the protesting man's words. "Our ancestors are served well. Bow your heads."

The patriarch glances at the rows of children at the children's table. "You children close your eyes and bow your heads, too." He can barely see their faces let alone their eyes but he waits a second or two to give them the chance to obey.

I see the Turtle shiver in confusion. She's sitting between two older children. She closes her eyes and clasps her hands together. I grew up in a family more Catholic than hers and my image of myself at that age cannot match the holy one I have of her. The Little Turtle has her eyes shut and I can see her thoughts. She thinks everybody in the world has closed his eyes and is waiting for something to happen. Only Old Gchachu knows what it will be. She peeks to see if her brother Albion has his eyes closed. He does. She closes hers again. Old Gchachu clears his throat.

The old man begins to speak in a chanting voice, saying words about the Lord God and the Sun and the Moon and the Earth. He asks these things to listen to him. Then he appeals to them, "Receive our thanks to the souls of our ancestors for this food which we are about to eat for the nourishment of our bodies. Dear

Ancestors, be with us always in your wonderful spirits and knowledge, be in our hearts, bless us with water and corn, give us the seed we need to make Mother Earth feed us so that we may live long, healthy lives in the spirit of you, our Great Ancestors. Amen."

They all repeat his last word. When I was a kid I thought "amen" meant it was time to be happy again.

You can see the Turtle peeking to see if it's time to open her eyes again. I used to do the same thing at Hopi when the priest stopped praying. One was never sure if it was going to be a full stop or a half one.

The Little Turtle turns to look at the daughter who looks old enough to be a grandmother. The grandmother-looking-daughter speaks. She says a long prayer in Zuni. The Little Turtle watches the grandmother-looking-daughter speak these words she has heard her other grandmothers speak. The Turtle notices that the other children and the grown-ups too still have their eyes closed. For opening hers like this, she expects to be punished but nobody says anything. If nobody sees you do wrong maybe wrong doesn't count. She stores away this discovery for future reference. She sneezes in her plate. She looks over at Marelda in fear. Her mother had always told her to cover her mouth when she had to sneeze. This time it had come out before she could catch it.

The women serve the men first then the children then themselves. Painted Turtle waits for the big wooden spoon to plop into her bowl. She looks at her father Waldo who is chewing a locust chrysalide. While she's looking away, the steamy hot stuff is poured from the spoon into her bowl. She smells it before she sees it. When the pouring woman has gone, the Turtle gingerly sticks her finger into the oily surface. She licks her finger. I can see the face she makes. It is a lovely bewilderment at the distance

15

from which I watch. For her, though, it is torment. Her tongue seems to lose sensation. She takes up her spoon and fishes for one of the dumplings, hoping it will taste better. It bobs away like the head of a boy swimming in Spirit Lake. I managed better in my day.

The Turtle climbs down from her chair and goes to her mother who tells her to go back to her place. With her thumb in her mouth, she obeys.

An older girl next to her tells her to eat her mukialiwe. She looks at the slimy stuff in the bowl. Her eyes begin to cloud. She looks around for her Grandma Wilhelmina. She sees her on the other side unwrapping something wrapped in cornhusks.

The Turtle climbs down again and this time goes to her grandmother who asks her if she wants a bite of lepalokia. The Little Turtle says yes. The thing is held for her to bite. She does so. Grandma Wilhelmina now tells her to go eat her soup. She says: But it's green. Her grandmother says: It's good; eat it.

Chapter 3
The Seasons

I f you are a man it's hard to always know exactly how to write about a woman—even as a girl growing up. Yet you must try your best. You can see she didn't have much time to play with dolls: there were her little brother and her sisters; perfect dolls with real diapers.

And the trouble of herself. She had diarrhea and toothache. Even as she played tag and jacks she had to look forward to emptying the morning slopjar, helping to scrub the floor, fry the mutton, clean the skillets. Slice the onions.

Winter cold drove itself through the logs like nothing you can think of in the Southwest. They say a woman's body is warmer than a man's. Don't believe it. I lay beside her many nights when she was grown. I was warm and she was cold.

Did she color in coloring books by the stove in the deep of winter? She did.

She wanted to be a boy. Little wonder. Boys at Zuni could look forward to initiation. After that, after the visit with the men to the kivas, they stepped up into daylight like gods born out of the ashes of the dead.

She wanted a slingshot but her father told her girls didn't need slingshots. She didn't ask for a rifle. She didn't expect a bow and arrows.

Some summers were cold as winter.

It didn't matter that nothing immediately made sense. Her father picked her up in his pickup. She was about the size of a six-year-old but because she was on her period she figured she must be—at least in this frame—about twelve. He asked her to save some of her blood for the kiva. He told her that while she was at school a Mexican had looked upon a Zuni mask and died. The villagers drove three other Mexicans off into the hills. She rethought this. Her father was not speaking directly to her. He was saying this to her mother. She helped her father later put up a fence around their house. She held the nails. She helped her uncle and her father build a new ladder for her uncle's kiva. The solstice dances came. Anglos came to watch them. She had never before seen so many gathered in one place. She liked the lightness of their hair and eyes.

One winter her aunt—on her father's side—was selected to go up to the top of Corn Mountain to bring the winter flame back from the burning light there and her sisters and grandmothers and other aunts cleaned the winter stoves and fireplaces and ovens and fasted for four days and the sword swallowers that winter were wonderful as they held forth quite seriously in the plaza. Phew!—what a sentence!

In the spring the planting ceremonies started and this was a lot of fun for the young fast-growing Turtle. She got to dance, dance, dance. Everybody thought she was pretty. She graduated from being cute.

The harvest ceremonies came. The mudheads—children of incest—made the people almost die laughing. For her, laughing was a way of controlling the fear of these monsters.

When spring came, she jumped naked with the other girls into Blackrock Lake and in winter she ice-skated on it. She was old enough to remember some of these things. For instance, one winter, two men fought—using juniper-made swords—on the ice and one, wouldn't you know, lost his kirtle and everybody laughed. She was proudly wearing, as she watched, the new winter black dress and leggins her mother had sewn for her.

Her sisters came along and they were like her but when her brother came along, last, and different, he was a novelty. He learned to dance in the Muwaiye. She watched him, touched, dressed, undressed him. She got the sense that he was special, being made ready for something she was excluded from. Eventually she learned it was called kiva. There was talk about the things he must learn. One, he must learn to ride a horse. Two, strap a cinch. Three, hold the horn of a saddle. Four, drive a pickup. Five, herd. Six, survive herding with comic books. Seven, survive comic books with soda pop. Eight, survive Life with chewing gum. Nine, he had to learn to chant—his chanting seemed more important than hers. He was half her size but folks paid more attention to him. He became good at long prayers. She was ashamed of it but happy when she saw him whipped in the Plaza at his initiation. For years, she kept the image of his head stuck between Waldo's legs, on the occasion when he got the breath blown into his mouth: this was the noive's binan. She envied the manta he later got. And the kiva he was taken to after initiation: that act, its privacy, was one of the first acts to seal her off—into herself. Her brother Albion was held between Waldo's legs in the wagon race. She was with her mother and sisters—watching. That was life. Boys, without a doubt, were more interesting. She, therefore, began to think of them as such. They didn't have to squat to pee. And what else?

When her sisters were old enough to do it with her, she danced the virgin dance in the Sword Swallowers Ceremony. She, like her sisters and the others, was dressed in snow-white robes off one shoulder. She loved her peplum ruffles, her white, turned-up moccasins. She cherished her headdress of black fur with the feathers and the star-shaped turquoise tablita. She carried her wands proudly.

She was the first, in her seventh year, to see the Sun priest leave the village and head for the hills. But nobody believed her. The importance of it was lost. Many years later she wondered at the inability of her people to trust the word of a child. Unseen Hands had told her to keep her mouth shut. She had, despite watching for five successive mornings, waiting, expecting. They were going to go to that mysterious, sacred, forbidden, other-wordly lake—way away in another state. There, the travelers gathered yellow or white clay and packed it in jars. It was the stuff that she saw on the faces of Kaklo, Salimopiya, Hainawi, Kokokci, Siwuluhsietsa and the many, many other kachinas; she saw it on their arms, their legs, their feet.

When she saw the little boy—playing the fire god—strike the match, she was glad she didn't know him and that she didn't have to see him the next day in school. The match set fire to a field of brush which gave the villagers lots of smoke to make the rain clouds come and she listened for the sound of rain to start—she was sure she heard it although she felt nothing like it falling from the sky. With the fire set by the sun god, the restlessness of the villagers began to end.

I'm sure she only imagined it, but she was sure her father—at this point—took a jar of her virginal blood to the kiva where the warriors waited. They painted their faces with it. When the enemy came, they would be ready.

> A powerful priest
> who has the right mix

of tooshoowe and kyawawulaswe
in his sacred bundle
tells her his secret
the first word
He was on good terms
with Uwanammi
the rain kachina
the Sun Priest
those at the Beginning:
Siiwilu Siwa Suwilu Siyeetsa

Chapter 4
Sheep Camp

W hy is the Turtle in the storeroom? I had a map but it's limited. I can hear her sobbing. She listens to her father's voice—outside, in the kitchen.

The storeroom door opens and her father speaks into her darkness. He tells her to get her jacket because at night it gets real cold at the Kechipbowa sheep camp. She doesn't move.

He pulls her out of the storeroom.

She helps her mother pack the food and the goods.

The men sit around the table. Painted Turtle takes the hot bread and the fried mutton and onions and the boiled potatoes to them. They eat, Marelda tells her if she has to be a tomboy she better stay close to her father. Girls shouldn't go out there.

They leave at sunrise. You can see it the way I see it, coming up along the range. In the Southwest everybody knows the magic and the loneliness and the sorrow of it.

They got to Kechipbowa.

Her father and the other men and boys brought their rolled bedding in from the pickups and dumped it along the walls. A bee was buzzing around up near the ceiling.

The place was mildewed. Painted Turtle had one thing in her mind: the lambs. She wanted to hug each one as they were born. But already she knew most of them would be born in the night and a lot of them would be dead by day.

It was the next morning.

In the pickup beside her father, she rode about a half a mile over to the corrals which were east of the house. She walked beside her father through the huge place, entering first the main pen. Meanwhile, the hired hands, who were already there, could be heard bringing the sheep down from morning grazing to a lower area where they would remain till sundown. It's the same at Tewa—though we had few sheep. Painted Turtle knew the whole routine because she had listened now for weeks to her father talking with his brother and cousins about what they would do at camp. She followed her father as the other men scattered, going in various directions, back to the shearing pen area, which was empty like the main pen. She climbed up on the rear railing and peeked into the shade at the wide shearing floor with its strands of wool from last year. She kicked her feet and held on with her elbows. Through the west planks she saw a couple of wire-horses standing outside in the shade of the fenced horse corral. Their eyes were closed and each had their left hind leg cocked. She liked the dank, animal smells of this place. They were what she remembered best about it—next to the lambs. Her father called her and she jumped down and went to him. She followed him out through the doorway into the pens. She could tell he was just checking things. He shook the feed racks to make sure they were sturdy and he checked for holes. One of her uncles came in and told Waldo part of the west fence needed repairing and the gate to the main-pen needed another latch. She stood up on the fence and walked along the railing. Her father told her to get down.

She got down and went for a walk.

She saw one of her older cousins. He wanted to show her something. She followed him. On the west side of the main corral

23

they came to a place where a ewe and a goat and a lamb were tied with ropes to the fence. The cousin said they belonged to him. The lamb was only two weeks old and it was nursing at its mother's teats. The cousin said his father and uncle gave them to him right after his initiation. Painted Turtle felt envious; although she did not envy the beating she saw him get in the sacred plaza. I was not beaten at Tewa but I had to go on the rabbit hunt. I may tell you about that one day.

Painted Turtle asked the cousin if she could hug the lamb. He said sure but don't hurt it. She got on her knees and stroked its back. It tried to look around at her without losing its hold on the ewe's teat. Then it stopped trying to see her. She stroked its neck and tickled its ears.

This seems long, long ago. But I have the clearest view of her in that posture.

One of her father's cousins stayed at the house and when they got back at midday, he had dinner cooked. They all sat on the floor and ate fried bread which they used as spoons to dip into the stew the cook had spooned into their tin plates. After eating, some of the younger boys wanted to go out and practice driving the pickups but her father and his brother told them being at sheep camp was serious business and that they were here to work.

After dinner they drove back out to the corrals. On the way she asked her father if she could help with the lambing and he told her she could watch.

The pregnant ewes had been placed in one corral together. There were about eighty of them.

Those that had not gotten pregnant had been cut off by the hired hands and were earmarked to be watched for slaughter next year. She climbed up on the fence where they were and looked at them. She thought about mutton frying in the cast-iron skillet.

She got down and ran over to the corral of the pregnant. Four newborn lambs were feeding at their mother's teats. She stood there at the fence and watched. They were so eager!

She lifted her cotton shawl from her shoulders and wrapped it around her head. The sun was up in the middle of the sky and it felt extremely hot. It was early May.

She watched her father squat in the sheep dung and poke at a ewe's stomach. A cousin squatted with him. Behind her, a man in another corral was yelling at the dogies. Another cousin was hammering at a fence on the west side of the main corral and another inside.

She squatted beside her father who was now pressing the ewe's stomach. After a while she saw the tip of the lamb but she couldn't tell which end was coming out first. The smell was strong and fetid.

Sunrise. Boys herding sheep out of the main pen through the gate and up the path. She watched them leave. She tried to count the sheep but lost count. The ears were marked different ways. She knew her father's mark. She wanted to be a sheep, to bleat sadly. Old Roony barked up on the hillside.

She turned and kicked at the sand.

Her father and his cousins were again at the corral of the pregnant ewes. From the fence she counted eleven new ones. Some were half standing on wobbly hind legs, others on wobbly front legs. One was lying flat on the ground. She went and touched its head. Her father slapped her hand. It was bad luck.

Hot days, cold nights. Her father asked her if she wanted to go back. One of the cousins was about to drive back to the pueblo for more provisions. It was Saturday morning, end of the first week of May. She said she wanted to be a boy. Her father playfully socked her jaw and told her to get in the pickup.

She refused to get in.

She sat on the ground by the motherless lamb and the stubborn ewe. She petted the lamb for a moment but the ewe kept moving from side to side, dislodging the lamb's grip on her teat. The ewe kicked at the lamb. Painted Turtle spanked the ewe's rump. A cousin forced the ewe against the fence and held her like that till the little one came over and started suckling again.

I've seen this happen many times.

They took some of the sheep up a little south of Hampasawa where there was better grazing land. They all came back before dinner time.

The shearers gripped the sheep between their thighs and started with the neck, working down the back, then down the sides, clipping close to the skin.

She helped stuff the sacks.

The cousins loaded them on the pickups.

Chapter 5
Kwelele

S he rolls cornhusks to make her ears. I stick them on her
head one at a time. She makes a black face showing herself
with white crescent eyes. With my finger I trace her zigzag nose.

She makes the crouched dance motion of winter. The solstice
is near. She's old Kwelele. I trace the outline of her spruce collar.
She rattles her beads.

I speak to her:
You are in the Coyote Clan. This is your mother's house.
Before, it was your great-grandmother Mary Wind Place's, a Bow
Priest's daughter.
You crawl with your head stuck up. You get the turtle name.
You are counted on.

She earns the best grades. Sister Acklam says she draws the
best hummingbird.

I speak to her:
You run till you come to the base of Heshota Uhla near the
river. Here you beat your tiny fists against the ancient ones at
Kechipauan then at Kiakima then at Kwakina.

Chapter 6
Blood

S he felt the blood before she saw it. It was her eleventh
birthday. She reached down there and brought up some on
her finger. She ran to her mother, scared, thinking she'd hurt
herself. Her mother gave her a rag and told her that it was the
curse of being a woman. She also said it had something to do with
life itself. Her mother told her that long ago, santi inoo as they
said, the Bow Priests and the members of the Secret Council of
the Apithlanshiwahi kept close watch on this blood.

Painted Turtle went outside and sat in the abandoned car on
the other side of the road. She was dizzy with the thought of this
blood—her own. She had known deer blood and chicken blood
and turkey blood and rat and mouse blood and snake blood and
sheep blood and blood from a cut finger and from the inside of her
own mouth when her teeth bit into her jaw, but...

She sat there a long while. What had her momma meant by
curse? Why had the Bow Priests and the members of the Secret
Council been so concerned and were no longer concerned these
days?

She began to sing a song she made up as she sang. The feelings
she pressed into it were forever engraved inside the skin of her
face.

I am the crow gut
I am the coyote gut
I am the deer gut
I am the rabbit gut
I am the squirrel gut
I am the mouse gut
I am the fox gut
I am the woodrat gut
I am the raccoon gut
I am the skunk gut
I am the sheep gut
I am the weasel gut
I am the lion gut
I am the shrew gut
I am the badger gut
I am the bighorn gut
I am the lizard gut

Yowejhhheeeeeeeeeeee
Eeeeee   yaaaaaa he

Chapter 7
Rape

K eith Leekela of the Macaw Clan forced her into the cab of his pickup. He drove out near Towayalanne. That's what they call Corn Mountain. Keith Leekela twisted her arm behind her back. She was calling out for help but no one could hear.

He pushed her up a footpath to a mesa. He smelled of beetle dung. He had muskmelon stains on his shirt.

He forced her to the earth and cut her open with his hardness. He was the jagged edge of a sardine can. She cried out for her mother and grandmother.

He finished with her and opened a can of beer.

She attempted to leave and he tripped her. When she fell he laughed.

When he finished the beer he raped her again. As he pounded her he smelled of empanadita.

Keith Leekela finished her for the second time; drank two more beers and fell asleep.

When she was sure he was sleeping deeply, she crawled away and scampered down the mountain side. As she ran down the path in the light of the stars of the Ash Way, she feared her mother would kill her for being so late coming home from school.

When she got home she told her mother the teacher kept her after school to help with a display of student drawings and watercolors.

Later she went out to the abandoned car and quietly sang this song to herself:

> When I was a little girl
> I ran around Corn Mountain
> early morning at sunrise
>
> When I was just a little girl
> I ran around Corn Mountain
> My hornbells woke Tarantula
>
> When I was a little girl
> Tarantula caught me
> he split me open
>
> When I was just a little girl
> Tarantula took my moccasins
> He tried to wear my leggins

Chapter 8
The Crow Bride

C lose your eyes. Try to imagine this. She is dressed as the Crow Bride. Her black wings reach up from her shoulders above her head. She's watching the spectators through the narrow slits of her blue-black mask.

Painted Turtle is about to dance the dance of the emergence from the ancient kiva. She carries her yucca blade-whips in her right hand though she is left-handed.

The last girl from the school allowed to dance this dance made twenty-nine mistakes. The village leaders will not tolerate mistakes.

She's in line behind Chof, the antelope. His tail keeps brushing her. She's nervous. Her mother has told her she is too ayavwi to dance this dance. She knows her mother is up there on the roof watching. Painted Turtle keeps her eyes closed as she moves on sacred ground.

She knows the steps and the bends and the arm dangles and the stuttering impulses perfectly, but with people watching she is not sure she will not make a mistake.

She thinks of her grandmomma's legs. They must be aching by now. Grandma Wilhelmina Loaded-Shotgun Waatsa has said many times that her ladder-climbing days are over. Yet she continues to climb up for sacred dances.

The dance begins. As the Turtle dances in rhythm with the others, to still her nervousness she reinvents Grandma Wilhelmina's voice, hearing the old woman say she'll see all the sacred dances she'll ever need in the next world where Christ and the kachinas will let her watch from the comfort of a plush armchair made of silver and turquoise.

As the Crow Bride, the Little Turtle is the only dancer from the Coyote Clan. She carries this responsibility as though it were the size of a John Deere tractor.

Chapter 9
The Arrow

Not long after Painted Turtle adjusted to the menses's rhythm of twenty-eight days, Unseen Hands came and shot an arrow into her back.

I swear, rather than pain she felt a burst of joy.

Her Grandma Wilhelmina came running out to where Painted Turtle lay in the yard. Painted Turtle felt her grandmother pick her up and hold her against her bosom, a place of comfort. As she lay against her grandmother she felt herself leave her own body and go flying up to the sun. The heat in her body had consumed her and she felt completely free.

When her grandma pulled out the arrow, she blacked out. While out she went swimming in a red river and there were girls all along the embankment crying and screaming as red sea water gushed out of them, running in rivulets down the embankment into the river. Painted Turtle was the only one swimming. As she swam, her body separated into two parts. Each one was a woman. They were embracing each other as they swam upstream. They swam for a long time before they pushed away from each other.

I can't tell you for sure which one was truly she or if it mattered.

At some point much later the two women became one again and Painted Turtle as the single woman climbed out of the rose-colored water. A bear came out of the forest and began to chase her. But something was wrong: the bear ran like a man. When he caught her he ate her screams. Her fingernails became razor blades: with them she scratched him as he tried to throw her down. He withdrew and licked his wounds by a bush. In the night she found a cave to sleep in. All night long the wind whispered in her ear and the desert came alive with the talk of night beasts.

When she woke her grandma was there leaning over her, speaking softly to her, cooing her. It helped to ease the pain in her back. The old woman said Cipapolima was only a myth.

Like a bird that doesn't know it can swim, Painted Turtle dives into the lake for the fish. When she brings it up, it's a song. She sings it:

> My shell is tough
> I shall be tough
> Tough as my shell!

Chapter 10
Prayermeal

The Turtle's birth pains were blue circles lassoing her every thirty seconds. Everybody knew for sure now: she was having a baby. She knew everybody knew.

Paulette Hapodina, midwife to the clan, is shaving the hair from Painted Turtle's bumblebee. Painted Turtle's Grandma Wilhelmina grabs the hair, careful to pick up every strand. She will store it in a secret place or burn it.

In the old days they would hang you by your feet and make you tell an amazing story of your accomplishments as a witch before granting you freedom. If your story failed to entertain the priests, you were beaten to death with a club. Anyway, Old Paulette wants Painted Turtle to get on her knees in the traditional manner. She would embrace the Turtle from behind and squeeze to encourage labor. Long, long ago, Paulette tells her, a hole was dug in the ground to catch the discharge from both places. Prayermeal, you can be sure, was everywhere.

Painted Turtle refuses to get on her knees. She tells Paulette that getting on the knees is old-fashioned and that she wants to have her child the modern way. Paulette and the other women tell her she is possessed by the Devil and that she should have gone to the hospital where the rest of the devil-women gave birth.

She later described the scene to me in a way that caused me to cringe. She said she was impaled on the the tongue of her grandma and her bottom-end floated in the air with a bunch of old women trying to yank a set of twins out of her from the rear. The midwife spat an emetic into Painted Turtle's mouth as she screamed. Meanwhile the other women shouted, Kneel, kneel! Next they hooked the girl to a rope tied to a beam and yanked her; they forced the Turtle into a crouching position and forced her to hold her own aching head as they yanked at her. They meanwhile called on the powers. One blew only smoke at her shaved area.

Take it easy, Paulette told her. She now pretended to be modern, this Paulette, but the Turtle knew better. The old crone smelled of her own tennis shoes and pinon smoke and yucca suds and honeyed arrows and offerings galore and tenatsali flowers you wouldn't believe. Paulette took out a fetish and placed it alongside Painted Turtle. Even in her agony Painted Turtle noticed how much like a boy's penis it was. She knocked it off the bed with her fist. Some of the women cried out, covering their mouths.

Old Paulette tells Painted Turtle she's gonna have twins. The Turtle can barely hear the old woman she's so crazed with pain. The respected midwife says the Turtle is about to give birth to Mokwanosana. The Turtle could not care less.

The girl's labor is hard. She turns when she senses they are not having any luck with her. She turns on her stomach again and Old Paulette straddles her, pulling at the top of the Turtle's swelling. From the corners of her eyes she can see Grandma Moira Crow Dog sprinkling prayermeal around the bed. The Turtle thinks: I'm dying and she's sprinkling prayermeal around my bed. She can hear the other old women fumbling and scraping around the bed, making their worrying sounds. Meanwhile, Paulette urges the Turtle to push. The girl pushes. And pushes. As she pushes she curses all ulani, all talaki.

Some of the old women had gotten tired and had gone home. Painted Turtle's momma sat by her, along with both grandmothers. Paulette stayed there too. Paulette ate mutton and mashed corn as she waited through the long night. The first thing the Turtle saw when she opened her eyes, after the pain spun away deep within her, was Old Paulette sitting in a corner, wiping her lips and rolling a cigarette. She watched Paulette smoke the cigarette with all the ceremoniousness of men consecrating a well-planned cornfield. The Turtle knew nobody knew she was awake. She wanted it that way. She watched Old Paulette as though she was some sacred figurine. Normally the old woman smoked a corncob pipe like other old women but now there she was treating herself to the speciality of men! At a certain age down the road the old women did that and did it well. The Turtle watched Old Paulette pass the cigarette to Grandma Wilhelmina.

But they weren't just twins. And this is the unusual part. The women went away to eat leaving one old woman with the Turtle who drifted off to sleep again. She was tied down with a squaw-belt. On her stomach she couldn't breathe with the full power of her lungs. The buckle bit into her back. The rolled blanket was above her abdomen. This was of course a dream she was having. She beat her fists in the dirt, kicked at the bushes. She was naked in the sandstone of a mesa. Somebody tightened the buckle. She cried out. Grandma Wilhelmina rubbed the sweat from the Turtle's head. The Turtle saw her mother Marelda holding the twins: except they were not boys; they were...

> Her sons were upside-down
> inside her, arms curled around
> their heads, sleeping
> the sleep of the cervix,
> breathing the sleep
> of primipara,

38

        dreaming the eternal dream
        of the uterus

        They were upside-down
        floating in her moonlight
        in her sea, swaying
        darkly in the pelvis grip
        attached to the placenta
        waiting silently

The rats and the coyote came at the same time to eat her flesh, to tear her to pieces. The Zunis sent a search-party out to find her stray bones. On the fourth day, her father went into the Plaza and held up a skull. He announced it to be her remains. But he was wrong: it was the head-bone of a girl dead many years. So the scalp dance was prepared in the Turtle's honor. Meanwhile, the twins were taken into the bosom of the village—and treated well: damned and adored at the same time. Cursed and revered, their dead mother's memory was blessed in the kiva by the medicine men and the priests of the Coyote Clan. They prepared for the ceremony. They gathered around the stove in the center and watched the smoke drift up through the skyhole. They began to chant, praying for the curse to be lifted from the people. They prayed hard. They danced till they were finished dancing then they sat around the stove again and passed a sacred cigarette around, smoking it slowly and respectfully. Then one of them brought forth the skull thought to be that of Painted Turtle and placed it near the stove where they all could view it. The skull spoke softly, as in a dream, of the glory of the ancient past. When they fell asleep and the fire was low, the Spirit of the twins came in to make sure these men were actually asleep and not pretending. That Spirit, satisfied that they were, then flew out into the forest to find the true remains of its mother. Its true father, the Supreme Toda, guided it. It found her bones and brought them back to the people.

> Reality is losing touch
> with the pain
> caused by the nail
> driven into the crutch
> you use to prop up your soul

It was hard for her to know when she was asleep and when she was awake. She felt her fingers aching as though she had played the guitar for six hours nonstop. When she tried to cry out, her vocal cords burned like the morningstar appearing at dusk.

> Her father could not hunt
> She could not go to funerals
> She had to be very careful
> She could not eat venison
> Her mother guarded the night

The Turtle fell asleep again. She was encircled by a spirit. She saw the spirit come down from the moon. The spirit lifted her up and took the pregnancy out of her and the pain with it. Painted Turtle felt her womb deflate. The spirit told her that she would not have to squat over a hole in the ground. As she is dreaming she is relieved that the birth has not taken place yet. At least this means the boys, when they are born, will be boys and not—not, uh, puppies. But how can the pregnancy be over and no infant in sight? Only the pregnancy itself then has come out and it is pure as air and light: it floats off in the six directions.

When the spirit left she looked down and thought she saw her womb hanging out and she thought she was dead, then some of the old women came back from supper. The Turtle woke.

Grandma Wilhelmina again spread prayermeal around the bed; the old woman pressed a handful of the ground corn into Painted Turtle's hand. She commanded the Turtle to throw it up and

40

around. Scatter it, she said. The Turtle was almost too weak to lift her arm but she managed to sling the meal. Painted Turtle groaned with discomfort. Paulette, who came and stood beside Grandma Wilhelmina, mumbled something about the young Indians not respecting the strength of the old ways.

Sometime in the middle of some night, after about thirty-six hours of labor (the Turtle told me), old Paulette cried out, "Atiikya!" and the others cried, "Hanahha!" and Paulette shouted, "Holy Jesus! she's giving birth to bear cubs! Look at these heads." The Turtle heard Marelda scream. The grandmothers began to weep. Some of the old women ran away, hastily explaining that they feared being touched in some way by the Devil.

The fear was abated when the cubs, upon being cut completely free of the Turtle, turned into twin boys. The grandmothers and Marelda and Paulette and two of the women gingerly touched the infants to test what they saw. They were human boys all right.

Her Grandma Wilhelmina wiped the sweat from Painted Turtle's forehead, cleaned the snot from her top lip.

Under normal conditions Keith Leekela's mother would have been there to take charge of the newborn infants, but it was Grandma Wilhelmina and Marelda who helped Paulette clean them and wrap them in a Navajo blanket.

When this was done the women prayed for the health of the boys and the safe recovery of Painted Turtle.

Grandma Wilhelmina whispered into the Turtle's ear, "You are blessed by the Mother of Dawn. I know the truth. Don't let these old witches scare you." And she kissed the girl's wet cheek.

Chapter 11
A Paper Uniform

Soon after the twins were born Painted Turtle went to work assisting nurses at the Zuni Hospital. If you've seen the place you know why it looks the way it does: it was one of those facilities built after the war.

Because it was a temporary job she had to wear a paper uniform. She felt odd and awkward. People camping in trailers out to the right of the parking lot used to come out to watch her walk down the road.

The boys were staying awake nights and she wasn't getting much sleep either. In the night she'd wake to find bells on the ears of one and a wooden beak jutting from the face of the other. When they cried and couldn't be silenced by her nipples, she sucked them to sleep.

The hospital collected a lot of strange people. One woman wearing a red feather was determined to follow her husband into death. When Painted Turtle took the woman her pills she couldn't find her because she became invisible in daylight. Only the night nurse could give the woman her pills. The woman refused to sleep facing west. Nobody could figure out why. When they turned her west she turned back east. In her sleep she kept mumbling something about wearing out four of forty pairs of moccasins just crossing the cactus desert trying to get to her dead husband.

On her lunch break Painted Turtle would take her guitar outside and sit in the shade and play. She had a cheap guitar then. She made up songs and she sang cowboy songs and Indian songs she knew. Sometimes she would fall asleep while playing. She tried to play like Prince Albert Hunt and sing like the Herrington Sisters. She used to hear them on the Texas radio station at night when reception was good. She practiced on things like "Home on the Range" and "Woopee ti-yi-yo." She felt more protected while playing, even in a paper dress, protected by Unseen Hands. She fell in love around this time with an etching by Gustave Dore she saw in a magazine. It was of a scene of Gypsy musicians on the outskirts of Granada. During her pregnancy she had not been able to play a lot because it had been difficult to hold the guitar properly, but now she made up for lost time at lunch time.

She worked at the hospital only about three months. They were kind, she thought, to keep her on that long since she was clearly not a good assistant and an obvious daydreamer.

She meanwhile was having a hard time keeping the boys out of trouble. They were beginning to crawl and were wrecking things. Everybody in the family had to watch them constantly.

Jobless and under her mother's scrutiny, Painted Turtle became too depressed to play her guitar or to sing. A member of the Council of the Gods came to her one night and, leaning over her bed, told her to act swiftly or she'd go crazy in this house. Pawtiwa clacked his wooden beak in her face and wiggled his top feather. He wiggled his huge fuzzy ears and whistled, making that sound that had scared her when she was a young child six years before. Pawtiwa went away but he returned on another night with a winter chill centered around himself which she could not long bear to feel. She drove him away with her indifference.

43

It must have been around three in the morning when she got up one night and took Bruce and Bryce out of their crib which was right by her bed in the same room where she and her two sisters slept. Yolanda must have been about ten and Lupe nine. The Turtle was careful not to wake them. She held one boy on one hip and the other on the other. With them like that, she tiptoed outside. It was cold. High winds were pouring down from the western hills. The boys didn't cry.

The Turtle walked right down to the Zuni River, which was only a few feet from the front door, and got down on her knees with the boys and held them by the neck and ducked their heads down into the water.

She held them like that till a hand yanked her by the shoulder. The force of the hand was so powerful that Painted Turtle lost her hold on the boys. She turned and looked up. The person behind her was Grandma Wilhelmina.

Chapter 12
The Red Cloud
Peace Crusade

They threw her in the mental ward of the Gallup Indian Medical Center the day after she tried to put the boys out of what she called their misery. Doctors from McKinley came over to look at her. Hospital Drive is a long way from Nizhoni Boulevard. They asked her why she wanted to kill her sons. She told them because they would have been better off.

Apparently they thought she was crazy.

After a few days here she lost her sense of humor and she began to fear that her sanity might go next.

In the same ward was a big Sioux who claimed to be a descendant of Red Cloud. Her spirit, she told Painted Turtle and the other women, was born at the Fetrerman Massacre and at the Wagon Box Fight. The big Sioux used a lot of vulgar words and chewed tobacco. Painted Turtle thought she was awful. One woman, a Hopi, told the Turtle that behind the big Sioux's back the other women called her Ground Rat.

The Turtle figured a good way to stay sane was to play crazy like these other women were doing. She began to watch Ground Rat.

One afternoon Ground Rat came to the Turtle in the coffee room and told her that the Red Cloud Peace Crusade was going to strike that night. "If you don't wanna take part just stay in bed." The Turtle wasn't sure what any of this meant but when the lights went off at ten she crawled under her cover as usual. She was a little corn-worm hiding in an ear.

The nurse was down there in his station reading a gun magazine. You could beat a drum in that coyote's ear and he would not lift his eyelids. He was stoned all the time. But he was the nicest guy they had on the staff.

Just minutes into the darkness, the Turtle heard them coming out of their beds and felt goose bumps break out all over her body. She peered through the darkness and saw a herd of fat Navajos and Hopis led by Ground Rat, silhouettes all. They crouched forward as they tipped on toes with arms extended and palms down and fingers ready like claws. The Turtle's heart beat like a gray fox running in her chest.

She heard the first attack.

It was followed by a short, cut-off screech. Obviously a hand went over somebody's mouth.

This was followed by sounds of muffled cries, struggle and scuffling—flesh pounding flesh. These were the sounds of a blanket party. The Turtle figured Clara the Zuni and Sandy the half-breed were getting it: Ground Rat hated both.

These sounds continued for maybe ten minutes before the lights went on and the nurse came running up the aisle. A moment after the lights came on the alarm went off and this meant that in seconds other nurses from other wards would come running to help. The gun magazine-reading nurse was quickly joined by these others. The Turtle watched them from a sitting position in her bed. They found two women struggling on the floor under blankets. They dragged the two hysterical women up and quickly got them into straitjackets and just as quickly carried them out of the ward.

The next day the word was that in the night Clara the Zuni and the half-breed had flipped out and had to be taken away for emergency shock treatment.

The Turtle felt that her silence was cowardly. Clara the Zuni and the half-breed were subsequently thrown into the Soft Room.

After two months here the Turtle began to fall in love with her doctor and this told her it was time to go. He was East Indian and his name was Sreenivassan. This love business had to be the first real sign of derangement. His family originated in a place called Kerala. She told him it sounded Zuni. He was planning to go back there to work in the hospital to help poor people. The Turtle dreamed of going with him. Finally, when he only smiled patiently at her innocent expression of love for him, which was not made very directly, she knew that she was just another appreciative patient. She felt rejected.

Doctor Sreenivassan told her she needed to adjust to the outside world again and quickly. He did not tell her she needed to go back to her sons. He did say that whether or not her sons live or die was not her decision to make.

Chapter 13
Pickup

The minute she got in the pickup she knew she had made a mistake. Hadn't she learned from the rape not to do this? The two guys were reeking of booze. She was by the door and the one in the middle put his arm around her and tried to feel her breasts. She knocked his hand away. He tried to unzip her jeans. He and the driver laughed derisively at her anger. She demanded they stop the pickup and let her out; but the driver wouldn't stop. He reached across his buddy and patted her cheek, making a tut-tut sound to show her how deep his scorn was. The one next to her giggled.

The driver began to slow down, getting ready to turn off Thirty-six onto a dirt road a little south of Whitewater. The Turtle made up her mind to try to jump out at the turn even if it killed her. There had to be a better way to get to Gallup to look for work. The driver shifted to first.

Meanwhile, Painted Turtle gave the middle guy a hard elbow in the side and another quick one in the neck, opened the door just as the pickup began to make the turn.

She leaped out into the scrubgrass, rolling over into a gully that separated the road from the cornfield.

She watched the pickup move on a few yards before coming to a complete stop alongside the road. They would try to come for her but they would have to run harder than a scared coyote to catch her.

With scratched arms, bruised elbows and knees, she scrambled to her feet and started trotting the short stretch back to Thirty-six. She heard them behind her, cussing and coming.

When she gained the hard surface, she literally was flying south, her oxfords hardly touching the cooling pavement. She didn't even have to look back to know that they were losing ground. Unless they went back to the pickup and drove after her they would have no chance at all. She knew that even if they did that there was still hardly any chance of them catching her. She had become as light as guitar music, as elusive as a song.

After several minutes of intense running she knew they had given up and had turned back. Up ahead she saw the beginning of the footpath she would take. No pickup could be driven onto it safely or sanely.

Early that same evening her youngest sister Lupe came running into the house and announced that she was going to be married to a boy named Felix Boone of the Corn Clan whose father was a farmer and sometime sheepherder. It was surprisingly easy for the Turtle to make the shift from anger and outrage to celebratory gaiety.

The courtship period was untraditionally short. Three months later the Turtle's family went with Lupe to the yard of the Boone home. Grandma Wilhelmina handed over a few pieces of jewelry and Marelda surrendered three jugs and a rug. These things were given to Felix's mother. In the yard there was a big jug and a straw chair facing it. Mrs. Boone sat on the chair and Lupe kneeled with her head over the jug. In this manner, Mrs. Boone washed the girl's hair with yucca soap. The woman's hands were thick and strong. She massaged Lupe's scalp vigorously. The Turtle watched with a crisscrossing of feelings; she could not separate one from the other. She and members of both families stood in respectful silence, watching the hair-washing ceremony. One of Mrs. Boone's daughters brought fresh water. Lifting it up in cupfuls, Mrs. Boone poured it over the top of Lupe's head. Then she dried the long black hair with a soft cotton towel. Meanwhile, Marelda, who was sitting on a matching chair with Felix on his knees before her holding his head over a similar water jug, washed the bridegroom's hair in the same manner.

So far, so good. After the washing, the two families ate the marriage mush from the marriage basket Marelda had brought with her.

That same day, Felix and Lupe moved into the old bedroom Painted Turtle and her two sisters had shared when they were children and the Turtle and her boys moved into the big storage room off the kitchen. It was cleared out and beds were put in.

Chapter 14
Expectations

She was tired as Yamuhakto carrying an armload of wood; tired from walking. She walked over to Coal Avenue again and again, looked in the storefront windows at the Indian jewelry in the pawnshops and gift shops.

At an intersection she suddenly forgot what the colors of the streetlights meant. At green she stopped; on red she began to walk. She was nearly killed by a Ford pickup.

She went over to Dean and sat on a bench in the Greyhound Bus Station. She watched the people go and come. Under her breath she made sounds like bluehorn makes, hoping for good luck. She imagined a big bird sitting alongside her. She feared it as much as she trusted it.

The man at the Amigo Motel on Sixty-six that morning said he would pay her fifty cents an hour to clean rooms and make beds. She figured she could make more babysitting.

She had also applied for the elevator-operator job in an office building but they had just hired a Navajo girl.

A priest needed a girl to sweep the church and his sacristy but she couldn't get in the church to talk with him because the door was locked.

On Aztec, out near the railroad office, a coffee shop boss told her to check back next week. He'd just hired a girl from Twin

Lakes but she might not work out.

She left the bus station. As she walked, she was Muluktaka. Snow flakes decorated her neck-plumage. It was a hopeless autumn. From a record shop loudspeaker Tex Ritter was singing "Moon Over My Shoulder."

At Woodrow Drive she saw the help wanted sign.

She went in. Her expectations were like the wings of sacred Mongwa.

Chapter 15
Difficult Circumstances

I t was winter and she was wiping the bar. There were two customers at it when her father came in.

She knew right away he was a little drunk when he said he wanted to tell her his life story. She placed a Coors in front of him and continued to nervously wipe the bar around his mug. It was a good thing Mister Fletcher wasn't here. He did not like for the relatives of help to come in while help was working.

Waldo said his story was a gift he wanted to give her for her forgiveness. He added that he didn't know why he needed her forgiveness.

She was ready as she was going to be under the difficult circumstances.

He talked in a Nawisho voice, as though he had a great black beard hanging heavily from his jaws. She could nearly imagine giant snowflakes spotting his eyebrows and nose. His voice was high and scary and bird-like and low as it varied in tone and she listened to the man who was her father as he transformed himself into words. He reminded her that he had come from a well-to-do family. He had taken kindly to living in Wilhelmina's house. He never questioned customs. He told her he loved her and his other children. He loved his wife and his mother and his mother-in-law. He wanted her to have everything, especially a good education.

When she was born he and Marelda had planned a wonderful future for her. But the other children had come so fast one after the other and the drought came. Sheep were lost. He told her she had been a sickly child and when tribal medicine failed the other kind was expensive but they spent what they had on it. Yolanda was also sickly and had to be taken to the hospital at Black Rock many times. Everybody in the clan tried to help the family during these lean years. The women made clothes for the children. Her clothes were passed down to Yolanda and when Yolanda outgrew them they went to Lupe. She told him she remembered. By the time Lupe was born she had dresses and leggins and mocassins waiting for her. He said he had done the best he could under very trying conditions. Half the time there was no grazing land even when he and his cousins had plenty of sheep. Often he sold at a loss. In the summer of 1940 when she was just a tot, he said, his sheep came down with a disease that wiped them out. He watched them drop dead in the corrals and in the fields. Had it not been for Wilhelmina's jewelry-making they would not have pulled through that winter. At least she had her license and sold the things she made through shops in Gallup and at the trading posts on the reservation. She had gotten hers before the Agency started charging so much for them. By the fifties you couldn't get started unless you had about seven hundred bucks. Nobody at Zuni ever saw that kind of money back then. He said the family was lucky if it saw five dollars a month. Sure, he had credit at the posts because of the sheep but even that got cut because of the loss. He said he used to pray in the kiva for better luck. He almost lost faith. Even the little garden out front had betrayed them. But he kept coming back to the problem of the sheep loss. He said the original herd belonged to her Grandma Wilhelmina. When he married her mother Marelda he took charge of two hundred head.

But after the bad luck he had only about seventy-five and even these were lost in 1940. Most Zunis swore by corn but you could give him the gentle sheep any day. He liked always to go out where they grazed and to just watch them and smell them.

His rambling talk made her nervous. She kept watching the door for Mister Fletcher. He was due any minute. But she could not think of a way to ask her father to leave.

He drank his Coors then talked again. He wanted to know if she remembered going that time to sheep camp when she wanted to pet all the newborn lambs. She assured him she remembered. He told her she was a child pretty as peaches on the trees in Spring. He bragged about being a better shearer than his brother and all of their cousins put together. He sheared two hundred sheep a day while the others were lucky to get half that amount done. He also bragged about being the best overseer of the lambing. He said that during the season the lambs were coming all hours of the night and day and somebody had to be there at all times because of the birth-problems plus the lambs often got mixed up and nobody could tell which was which except when you saw the ewes the lambs went to but if a ewe died and a couple of lambs died it got pretty complicated. He often stayed all night in the corrals for these reasons. He laughed to himself. He then drained the beer from the bottom of his bottle. He laughed again then looked at her. She stopped wiping the bar top. He told her she was a tough girl and always had been. She liked sheep camp better than washing dishes. He said he used to wish she had been born a boy because she was better than all the boys in the clan and much tougher. When he said this she thought of her brother Albion playing chase-the-stick that summer when he was supposed to be baling fleece.

During this moment of silence the door opened and Mister Fletcher came in, shaking the snow off his big boots.

Chapter 16
A Hundred
and Twenty-One

I t was a week after her father stopped in to give her the gift of his story. Mister Fletcher came in bringing a rush of freezing air with him. He stopped just inside the door, stomping his rubber boots on the mat. She watched him bristle and shake his head. He was early: he hardly ever came in before five.

One customer had a half-empty mug in his fist. The Turtle went down and asked the guy if he wanted another one. The man said no. He had a face like a mudhead. She went back to the other end of the bar and started wiping it.

Mister Fletcher came over behind the bar and told her he wanted to talk with her. His friendly twinkling eyes had changed. The change in him caused her to turn into a scared little girl, ready to run from the Shalako. They were out of earshot of the lone customer.

He stuttered as he spoke. He had to let her go, he said. He said it was because she had lied about her age. He told her she was seventeen, not twenty-one. She wanted to tell him she was a hundred and twenty-one if a day and ready to spend the rest of her life at the bottom of the earth, suffering and knowing joy, ready too to soar above the earth forever knowing the light and the lightness of moving along on wings, that she was old enough and young enough always and that her age had never started and never stopped and never would start and never would stop, that he did not understand, that she did not either, that none of it made any sense, the rules were one thing here, another there, that people were either trusted for a while or mistrusted then without notice often lost to both trust and mistrust and vanished forever. She wanted to tell him he was wrong not to believe in her but she instead listened to him express his disappointment in her.

She was unable to look into his old sad face because she was learning that age wasn't the same thing as wisdom, as the old ones at Zuni had insisted. He told her he might have lost his license were it not for a friend in the police department who chose to believe he had not willfully violated the law by hiring a minor to serve liquor. Again he told her how disappointed he was in her lying.

She said she was sorry. She put on her cloth coat and went out into the cold. She would get to the reservation in time to see the Shaliko dancers being led across the river into the pueblo. Snow was falling lightly.

Chapter 17
Night Vision

Being eighteen got into her dream like the snowstorm. It came suddenly like a physical blow or like having holy water sprinkled by a Franciscan priest onto your face. But it was real and hard as your own chongo-knot. Real like the sound of the angelus. The dream woke her like the alarm of smallpox.

She got on her knees slowly, careful not to wake the twins, to see the snow out there in the blue silence. A crowded bed now, with them so big at five. She didn't expect to see the northern lights, not even stars, certainly not stars. In the past summer she had searched and waited for northern lights but they never came this far south. Some said they did but you had to have the special eye.

> They told me I needed
> to attend the Indian school
> but I was a dropout
> before I started
> They told me I needed
> friends at NCAI and OEO
> but I told them
> just as it is rude
> to eat too much
> it is rude to doubt
> too much

She gazed long at the frozen night landscape, unable to see distinct objects: the old car by the river; not even Corn Mountain. Her eyes burned with night vision. She longed to lift her old guitar from under the bed and play but doing such a thing in the dead of night was out of the question.

Slowly, she lowered herself back into her place on the outside and dropped her left arm down to the floor. She reached under the bed and felt the cool wood of the instrument, then touched—with the lightness of an old man lowering a burden-strap from his forehead to rest his bundle of firewood—its strings. The sounds they made were so delicate she could not hear them.

Chapter 18
The Barking Bird

O ld Gchachu told her to sit on the floor at his knee. When she hesitated he said that the wisdom of an old rain-maker shouldn't be questioned. He was the one who called for thunder. Uhu ehe yelu. Aha ehe. He told her his spirit was beautiful. She counteracted his claim by telling him she was a singer and a maker of music. At this point she began to suspect she might be dreaming this. He closed his eyes. They were apparently in the sitting room of his house. It did not look like the house of Wilhelmina Loaded-Shotgun Waatsa. She folded her arms and patted her left foot on the floor while resting on her right; then she sighed, as though in resignation, then eased down into a sitting position on crossed legs. She watched him through squinting eyes. He rested his arms on the arms of the chair. He told her, out of the blue, that he was the leader of the party that went to Washington with Zuni grievances which he expressed to the Commissioner of Indian Affairs. He also met that good BIA man John Collier. Kokokei sang a song of Gchachu's success as he danced in the summer dances that year long ago. She was tempted to ask him to get to the point, but he was an old man and the leader of the clan.

Old Gchachu patted the top of her head. He told her she was pretty then he said he wanted to enter her spirit, to raise her spirit to the level of his own, to help her fulfill her promise.

She told him she had no song for him. Go, old man, and make thunder elsewhere. She got up.

He said he would call upon the punitive kachinas to punish her and she invited him to go right ahead.

He began to chant: Hainawi Hainawi Hainawi Homatci Homatci Homatci Temtemci Temtemci Ahute Ahute Ahute. As he called they appeared mysteriously at the window, tapping gently on the glass. They were hideous; worse than she remembered!

Old Gchachu whistled like one of the Saiyalia on the way to a winter house. As though his whistling was a signal, a Saiyalia opened the window and climbed into the room.

Painted Turtle moved toward the door, ready to run.

A few of Saiyalia's eagle-tail feathers fell from his rear end. The white horsehair of his mask was wet.

The Saiyalia danced around the room, coming menacingly close to her. She grabbed the doorknob but it wouldn't turn.

Old Gchachu commanded the Saiyalia to stop. In a language she did not understand the old man talked gently to the dancing-bird.

She shook the doorknob as the Saiyalia again—this time slowly and cautiously—approached her.

When he was close enough for her to feel his feathers he bent down and whispered, telling her she came into the world for a noble cause but that she had betrayed that cause and now must submit to the love-embrace that would cleanse her of her curse. The bird said he was her spiritual husband and that mating with him would also raise the curse from her sons.

She shouted for Old Gchachu to send the Saiyalia away but he ignored her.

Saiyalia leaped on her, knocking her to the floor.

61

She screamed.

As the Saiyalia tore at her clothes he clacked his beak again and again, barking the bark of Kanakwe: Huita! Huita! Huita! He shouted in her ear as she continued to scream. She reached down to try to divert his hand and its instrument. She touched a corncob. While this struggle lasted she was dimly aware that the old man had disappeared and that the punitive kachinas were still watching through the dark glass. She shuddered convulsively as she turned her face away from the tobacco smell of the Saiyalia's breath.

Chapter 19
The Smell of Ashes

H er sons, she said to her mother who was sitting in
Grandma Wilhelmina's rocker, by the rules should have
been initiated at birth but they were not. She told Marelda that
the hurt this caused had never gone away. She said she did not
blame the family; not even the clan, only Old Gchachu who obviously had given the order. But what was past was past. Keith's
mother could not have been called on to cuddle the newborn
twins—and who would want them committed to Leekela's kiva
anyway? She understood all the reasons why the initiation was
omitted. Old Lady Leekela was not the person to cut the cord
and to dab the wound with mutton fat and a wad of uncooked
bread.

The Turtle watched her mother's face.

Marelda kept right on knitting and her stern expression did not
change.

Painted Turtle smiled to herself. Besides, she said, laughing,
Old Lady Leekela probably would have buried my navel cord in
her own stomach rather than under that rock out there in the yard
by the oven where I first learned to bake.

Marelda gave her a sharp look. The Turtle liked the intensity of
it: it was rare. Marelda spoke softly, saying that she and her
mother Wilhelmina put her on the hot rocks and covered her with

a Navajo blanket when she was out of her mind. Wilhelmina prepared the boys and cut the cord and put the boys down beside the Turtle. Moira had wanted to rub dirt on the Turtle's navel where it was still raw but—Marelda said—she wouldn't let her. Her mother told her her milk wouldn't come at first so they thought they would have one of the other young mothers—two of the Turtle's father's cousins' wives were nursing infants—to nurse the boys. But the Turtle's milk started in the night.

The Turtle remembered the smell of ashes. In her mind these years later she could still see the women rubbing them on the twins and the moonlight and later when they were still doing it, she asked her grandmother to stop them because it looked to her like witchcraft but Wilhelmina, she remembered, said it was good luck. They kept doing it day after day, just the way they had done it to Albion just after he was born. She remembered watching. She didn't remember anything about Yolanda being born. They kept her out of the room because Waldo wanted a boy. And Lupe had been born in the government hospital at Black Rock. She had to be taken out through the stomach. Because of these circumstances Lupe hadn't gotten the rites. This fact, Marelda always reminded everybody, was one of the causes of her great sadness. Nobody had respect anymore for the old ways.

The Turtle remembered the smell of charcoal. Marelda had covered the twins' chests with it so that at night they would be invisible and therefore safe. Just as Marelda had done with her own children, she had seen to it that Painted Turtle's boys had a piece of turquoise in bed with them while they slept during those first very dangerous weeks. She also kept the lamp burning through the night.

Chapter 20
A Yellow House

S he drove to the wealthy part of Gallup out near the golf course and parked her father's pickup on a quiet street. On the radio Ray Price was singing "Cherokee Cowboy." She waited till he finished before she got out.

She walked along the quiet street. It was Susan Avenue.

She selected a yellow house without thinking about it. The front porch was green. She looked back over her shoulder. The Country Club back there was clean and quietly nesting in a plot of freshly cut blue grass: a giant white bird warming its chicks. She read the name above the knocker: "Carroll." She lifted the knocker and banged it against its cradle. She thought of turning to see if anybody was watching from across the street, spying on her from behind the lace curtains. She waited and there was no response.

Painted Turtle skipped down from the porch and trotted along a path to the back. I imagine she had no thought at this moment, no plan. She was all action. The door there was not locked. She let herself in. The excitement she felt was like that she had felt when her grandfather and her father began stories with "Many men's ages ago" and she knew something really exciting was about to happen. They were going to create a world of words for her. She was breathing the air of Turquoise Mountain, of Corn Mountain, of Sacred Mountain, of Towayanlanne! Ha ha waha!

She opened the door. Going in, she whistled a tune. She stepped into the kitchen, still whistling; perhaps it was a Carter Family favorite, "Bury Me Under the Weeping Willow."

A copy of a musty book was opened alongside a steaming hot bowl of chili. Somebody had just stepped out of the kitchen for a moment and was clearly planning to return and eat and read at the same time.

She lifted the spoon by the bowl and dipped it into the chili and brought the spoon to her mouth. She flicked her tongue at the chili. It was burning hot. She put the spoon down.

She went to the toilet. Here there was a shower and a bathtub and hot and cold water faucets and lots of tiny bottles on a counter and a dainty pink rug on the floor. It smelled better than your average outhouse.

After the toilet she wandered into the living room. The television was on with the volume turned off. A woman was crying and blowing her nose into a handkerchief.

Next she entered a room with a large table. There were six chairs around it. It looked like the conference room at tribal headquarters. A mirror on the wall to her left suddenly reflected her own image; her long black braids seemed blue in this light. Her dark eyes were just as blue.

She went to the mirror and lifted her arms. She lowered them, held them close to her chest, with thumbs inward close to her shirt. She made a fist of her right hand. Then she shot it down and out at the same time and ended the motion by almost touching the mirror. She looked at the expression on her own face. Made self-conscious by the river-depth of the mirror, she turned her back on it.

She entered a hallway. There she stood, looking around. It was

66

a tunnel of mystery. She was not sure she should enter it. But she was tempted by this mystery. Convinced that the best way to overcome temptation was by giving in to it, she began to walk—slowly, cautiously—into the semi-darkness of the hallway, fascinated by the possibilities it held.

Along the way she encountered one closed door after another. This went on for some time.

At long last she came to an opened door. She tiptoed over and peeked in. In the center of the room there was a bed larger than any she had ever seen.

Behind her, up the hallway in the living room, she could hear the woman on the television screen sobbing, sobbing as though her pain itself had turned the volume up.

Painted Turtle entered the bedroom. She stood still. She cocked her head, listening past the crying, straining for other sounds of the house, the family that lived here. Taking careful ceremonious steps she went to the side of the bed and just as ritualistically she undressed, leaving her clothes in a pile at her feet.

In one dance-step leap she was on the bed, then she stretched out to take a nap but sleep would not come. She kept her eyes closed and tried to lie perfectly still.

Finally, she left the bed, dressed, and quickly left the warmth of the house forever behind her.

Chapter 21
Gentleman John

He looked innocent enough to trust. He was probably eighteen, a year younger than herself. And there was a smartness in his face. It amused her that he would be her first. She could see he was having a difficult time getting up the courage to approach. She was standing in front of Sid's pawnshop next to the Amigo Motel's parking lot. He was a few feet away leaning against a metallic gold Valiant. It was a hot dry evening.

She waited patiently till his eyes met hers. When they did she held him and pulled him in with a slow smile that opened like the wings of a white-tailed hawk in the dry phase.

Careful to move her hips as she strolled over to him, she gave his eyes permission to move away, down her body, along the line of her breasts, across the expanse of her hips which were the two parts of a perfect motion.

When she closed the door behind them and smelled the roach spray of this Amigo Motel room, some of the edge of the game rubbed away. Asking for another room wasn't worth the trouble. She was a little girl who had thrown her jacks too hard. She looked at the boy standing nervously by the door. He seemed even younger. He asked her about the smell. She told him what it was and told him to undress and give her the money because she didn't have much time. Meanwhile, she was unbuttoning her blouse. She kicked off her pumps with relief. She had not yet learned to walk well in them. He had not moved.

She asked him his name and he told her Robert, which sounded as good as any. She stopped unbuttoning her blouse because of the look that came over his face. She thought he was going to cry.

She went to him. Had he changed his mind? He said no.

She felt the blow before she saw anything. Then she tasted the blood in her mouth before she knew she had been smashed in the face. She heard the thud of bone against bone. A streak of red light moved across her closed eyes.

She knew now, as she lay on the floor, that she was being kicked in the head. The shoe was hard and she was moving over to the edge of the pain where the darkness, like a cradle, began to bed her.

When she came back from that darkness, she was in a cold and bright place. She lay still till she had pieced together all of it that she ever was going to understand and remember. After a long time, she reached out for the leg of a nearby chair. She pulled herself to a sitting position. The fronts of her shirt and jeans were covered with dry blood. It wasn't clear yet whether or not she could stand or if it was worth the effort it would take.

Chapter 22
Segovia's Guitar

She was wearing the difficult pumps again and had her lips painted red. The jeans were so tight she could barely move.

She stopped under a street light. She was aware that some of the men in passing cars slowed down to get a better look at her. She lighted a cigarette and pretended to smoke it.

A big green Dodge stopped at the curb near where she leaned against the pole. The driver was no Robert: he was an older man, perhaps somebody's grandfather. He rolled down the window and asked her if she needed a ride.

She looked up and down the street and seeing no policeman, went over to the window. On the dashboard there was a little plastic figurine of the Holy Virgin; a dried rabbit's foot hung from the rear-view mirror.

The idea was to talk dollars first. Never forget that and never get in unless you think you can trust the guy and the question of money has been settled. Don't bother with an hombre who doesn't look clean and well-dressed. Skip drunks. Stay out of clinkers; avoid Mexicans and Indians. How had she learned the rules? Seemed to her she had always known them.

She asked if he was interested in some action and if it was worth twenty-five bucks to him. He didn't respond; instead, he asked her to get in because it was hard to see her and to hear what she was saying. She refused.

She turned to leave. He called her back.

She got in but left the door open.

He wanted to know if she was Navajo and she shook her head no then told him she didn't have time to chat. To herself she didn't sound like herself.

> Some things I will do
> Some things I won't
> I won't change the beds
> at a fleabag
> I don't wash windows
> I won't scrub floors
> Some things I will do
> Some things I won't

She gazed at the Virgin while he was telling her twenty-five was too much, that he couldn't afford it.

She made a motion to get out and turned back when she heard him groan an okay then she looked back and he was taking out his wallet.

> I come from the Zuni Reservation
> but not my lipstick
> I come from the Zuni Reservation
> but not my high heels
> I come from the Zuni Reservation
> but not my sweet smell

He handed her two tens and a five and she told him to drive down Sixty-six to the Amigo Motel. The room would cost ten. He said he thought they might use the car after parking somewhere on a dark street. That had been okay with the other Indian women he had been with.

She told him she didn't care what other Indian women found okay, that if he wanted to be with her he had to rent a room. Then he wanted to know why the Amigo Motel and she told him it was the only one she knew that accepted Indians.

The minute he stopped the car the grandfather-looking guy took out a badge and showed it to her and told her she was under arrest for prostitution. She laughed and told him he had a fine way of making a living, that she wished she could think of something as clever. He told her not to be funny. He handcuffed her just as another car stopped alongside them.

He held her elbow and escorted her over to the car where a policewoman sat in the passenger seat. The driver was in uniform and gave her a big smile as they approached. The grandfather shoved her into the back seat of the cruiser. He then slammed the door.

She was thankful for the darkness. She closed her eyes and thought of the guitar of Segovia she heard that morning on the radio. She had never before heard such a pure sound. She thought, I am as soft as that music but my shell is tough. She kept her eyes closed as she felt the car begin to move.

> The old folks said
> us Indians who went
> with men across the line
> were a disgrace
> We had fallen from grace

Chapter 23
Mary Etawa

The policewoman pushed her ahead of herself into the station which was vomit-gray and battleship-brown.

The Turtle was then steered into a small room with wired windows and scuffed benches.

She was left there for about ten minutes. At this point another policewoman carrying a clipboard came in and stood in front of her. She wanted to know the Turtle's name. But the Turtle's mouth wouldn't open. It was a conch shell.

The policewoman told her she wasn't going to take any shit from her. She wanted the name and she wanted it right now. But the Turtle's silence held.

The policewoman left the room in a huff and another one carrying the same clipboard came in a minute later. This was the one who had been in the passenger seat of the cruiser. She thought of telling the woman her name was Pocahontas but decided she wasn't that angry or that funny. Anyway, she was too tired to play.

> I dance
> with the crazy guy
> whose legs are goat legs
> He blows his flute
> at the shadow
> I cast

The policewoman asked her her name and Painted Turtle said it was Walk a Long Way; no, it was Bird Face; no, it was White Moccasins; no—

Lightning shot across her eyesight. Thunder did not follow. The policewoman nursed her hand as the Turtle gazed steadily at a fly on the upper wall. The policewoman called her a bitch. She banged her over the head with the clipboard then pushed her against the wall. The Turtle slid down to the bench and in this sitting position, looking up at the poor woman, said, "My name is Mary Etawa, born December 17, 1936 at Zuni Reservation. I attended Saint Anthony's before transferring to Zuni Day School. Worked at the hospital for awhile. I have two sons. My father's name—"

The policewoman slapped her and demanded the truth—said that she was going to be sorry if she didn't stop being a smartass.

The other policewoman returned and the two of them went to work on her. When they had her stripped and pinned against the wall and were breathing heavily into her face she knew they had trouble doing their work. These were not violent women, the Turtle thought. One or both might even belong to the Audubon Society. Perhaps the other one or both were president of the Gallup branch of the Catholic Daughters of America.

She told them her name really was Mary Etawa and she watched their faces. She saw the beginning of belief in those four eyes.

The one who had been in the car left and came back with a plastic bag and folded uniform, sheets and a blanket. She dumped the things into Painted Turtle's lap, picked up her torn shirt and the damp jeans and stuffed them into the bag. The other woman shook her head sadly. She said, "Don't you people ever learn—why do you have to be so difficult?"

Chapter 24
The Origins of Shame

The long dim room she saw before her was crowded with broken and spiritless and toothless and smelly shadows of women. One immediately came to her and asked her for a dime, another wanted a cigarette; a third one wanted to know what they got her for.

She followed the attendant to the empty bunk. Five or six bored inmates followed and stayed after the attendant left, watching Painted Turtle make her bed. One was leaning on a crutch, another was scratching the sores on her arms and legs.

The attendant went away and the Turtle continued making her bed. One of the women grabbed the other side of the sheet and began tucking it in for the Turtle. This woman introduced herself as Loren Sahwarita.

An attendant came in at ten the next morning and called out the names Loren Sahwarita and Mary Etawa and three other names. The Turtle with the other four women was escorted out of the detention room.

After arraignment, the Turtle left the court building with Loren Sahwarita.

They got off the bus at the Hershey Miyamura Overpass. Loren pointed below; said she lived beneath the bridge. The

Turtle knew what this meant.

She followed Loren down a dirt path into the arroyo. Immediately the stench of human waste swam into her nostrils. She followed Loren between the shanties. Flies buzzed at the piles of garbage and even at the small naked babies and children with swollen stomachs. A half-starved dog that looked like a coyote sniffed at the rear end of a two-year-old. Two pups were lying in the sun: she saw the outline of their ribcages through their pelts. A group of old winos was down at the water's edge sharing a bottle of Thunderbird. An ill-tempered boy fell into step with the Turtle and held a snot-crusted hand up to her, asking for money. She followed Loren past a group of young mothers sitting on the ground by a shack. Three of them were nursing infants. One had a whiskey bottle turned up to her blistered lips. Loren spoke to them and they mumbled return greetings. The path swung out along the river. They followed it, going toward the bridge, past an old man hammering a sheet of scrap metal to the side of his hut. The hammering caused the tar paper to fall off the other side. Ahead of her, Loren stopped to chat with a group of elderly women. The Turtle stood respectfully aside as Loren spoke with the women in Hopi.

Then they entered the shadow of the bridge and came to Loren's shack. It was built so that it leaned against the dilapidated one next to it. An old woman smoking a cigar squatted near the entrance. She looked up and tried to focus her rheumy eyes on the Turtle and Loren. Loren greeted the woman calling her Weekooty. She was Zuni. Old Weekooty, in a cracking voice, told Loren she'd fed the young ones her own cornmeal. She'd also kept them from the broken glass and the wine bottles. Old Weekooty gave out a crone's cackle, showing her purple gums. Her tongue was spotted black. The Turtle's empty stomach tried to erupt its acid.

76

She covered her face—trying to hide her gagging. Then she looked out over her hand and saw two small children. Snot hung from the youngest's nose in a long disgusting confetti-strip. He came trotting over to Loren and grabbed her dress. He started crying and sucking his thumb at the same time. The older child, a girl, followed. She gazed steadily at Painted Turtle, as she too took hold of Loren's dress.

Old Weekooty left and Painted Turtle followed Loren into the shack. She had to stoop. Inside, with the children still clinging to her, Loren apologized for the condition of her home but told the Turtle that she was welcome to stay and to also bring her twins to live here, if she wanted to. She gestured toward an empty corner and said that bedding could be placed there. Then in a sudden burst of rage and impatience, Loren knocked the children away. They crawled into a corner and hugged each other and whimpered and sucked their thumbs. The Turtle was embarrassed, confused, and made to feel an anger to which she could give no shape.

Loren lighted a candle and the dim light showed the place. The dirt floor was covered with straw and newspaper and cardboard. Against one wall was a ratty mattress. Loren told the Turtle she got the mattress when it was thrown out of a window of the Taft Hotel during a fire on the second floor. Loren placed the candle on a tin bucket turned upside down in the center of the shack. Overhead, Painted Turtle could hear the thunder of trucks and cars going across the bridge. She thought of her sons and looked at the children crying in the corner.

Loren said she was going to make some coffee but the Turtle told her it wasn't necessary. But Loren insisted and scampered about looking for a way to begin. The Turtle could not bear to watch. She closed her eyes and felt guilty for doing so. Without

77

knowing why, she felt shame.

> Sonahchi. How did shame come
> into the world? You can feel it
> crawling up your leg like a bug.
> The Turtle on the back
> of Tkianilona's head recognizes
> everybody at the ceremony,
> knows all the secrets.
> Shame came into the world
> through the back door.
> You know the story of the girl
> who goes out into the forest
> to have her baby so nobody knows.
> A deer carries the infant off
> to the mountain and he grows
> up in four days and comes down
> to save the people from death.
> Semkonikya.

Chapter 25
The Snake Girl

She knew from their breathing—and she could hear it well—she had the Snake Pit audience with her. Some of them might drop a dime in her basket on the way out. This feeling was like holding a frog, feeling its warmth and throbbing, in the hand. The strings of her guitar danced under her driven fingertips. When the audience wandered, the intensity of her refrain kept pulling it back.

> I'm the snake girl
> I wiggle for you
> I'm the snake girl
> I wrap myself around you

And she was carrying them on now into the guts of the song, where she wanted them to turn and spin and flip with her. This was the best justice she'd ever done "Snake Girl." With a rush of urgency she threw it out into their faces like happy-pies at a free-for-all. They were eating it up.

> I'm the snake girl
> I shake my gourd
> I'm the snake girl
> I cure the snakebite

She hit the strings harder and harder when she flung out the word "girl." Her high voice was dropping impossibly below her range.

She growled, grumbled, snorted, vibrating the glasses in hands and on tables. The oval stage beneath her also seemed to tremble from the low impact of her voice. She was driven like the great Valley of Flowing Water, old El Rio Grande del Norte, cutting its violent and beautiful way up through the parched land. She hummed the words into things with new curves, things that sent off sparks.

> I'm the snake girl
> I shake my rattle
> I suck out your poison
> I'm the snake girl

And again she beat her fingers against the old guitar as if it had harmed her, bitten her, and she was getting holier and angrier than anyone had a right to be.

> I'm the snake girl
> the desert snake
> is my father
> I'm the snake girl

And she brought the pace back slowly to where it had been in the beginning, but she was still racing with time and the frenzy of the song's own proposition was still there. She fell back slowly to this talking-pace where the words got softer, longer, slower. She put her tongue's curve to them, giving them some measure deep from her throat while she let her guitar notes whisper between these things called words which had found their way permanently into the room, even perhaps into its walls and the floor.

As she brought her song to its end she threw herself recklessly into its chances, its unknown possibilities, and as she ended it, she felt the audience knowing her, believing in her, and she knew beyond doubt she had pushed it out there, fully, like a hand or the whole body seeking to be embraced, understood, loved and feared at the same time.

Chapter 26
In a Tee Pee

A fter she made her debut in the cantina known as The Snake Pit she took to the road hitting one joint after another throughout the Southwest stopping where club bosses would let her perform in exchange for tips. All of this work took place before Peter Inkpen discovered her and became her agent.

She travelled by Greyhound and Trailways buses. The places that gave her space for peanuts faded together in no time: the Punta Tavern, the Costilla Lounge, the Rincon, the Ocate, Montezuma's Retreat, Stardust Country Club, La Hacienda, Club Dolphin, Sally's Entertainment Palace, Lazy L Club of the Lazy L Motel, Casa Lobster and Steak Nite Club, Club Dante, Dos Amigos Cafe, the Blackbird Cantina, many others; and the cities—Phoenix, Albuquerque, Taos, Valencia, Cuba, Venice—too got mixed up in her memory. But it was at Club Ranchito's in Gallup that she was discovered and later became a favorite and worked most often. Inkpen, who was scouting around, first saw her there.

She spent a lot of time gazing out of bus windows at dry unmapped land. The people she sat next to were at times in themselves worthy or unworthy of the trip. This one time she was on a Greyhound just after leaving Gallup, entranced by the changeless land in its harshness, on her way to Albuquerque on Forty when a

little girl in the seat next to her tugged at her sleeve. The girl asked the Turtle if she was an Indian. The answer was yes and the
girl tossed her blond locks from her eye and said she thought so.
The girl's mother, who was seated across the aisle, leaned over
and told the girl not to bother the lady. The Turtle assured the
mother that the girl was no bother. The mother smiled awkward-
ly. The girl waited till her mother was no longer looking then she,
in a whisper, asked Painted Turtle if she lived in a tee pee. No.
Then how did she live? She lived in a house. The minute the
Turtle said this she realized she no longer lived in a house. She
lived nowhere in particular; perhaps most often in motel or hotel
rooms. The girl wanted to know if Painted Turtle's house was the
kind with a stove and a telephone and a light bulb and a bathtub
and a sauna and a swimming pool. Well, not exactly. There were
chairs and a table. The girl said her name was Lenore and wanted
to know the Turtle's. Mary, the Turtle said. The girl spoke the
name. It was not an Indian name. The girl told Painted Turtle
that her teacher had taught them all about Indians: how they
make rain and grow corn and how they dance. The Turtle smiled
at the child then turned to look beyond the glass. There was the
Mesa Gigante. In minutes the bus would be moving through the
limited lands of the Canoncito. She had to pee and the next stop
was a long way along the road.

Chapter 27
Facing West

W hen Painted Turtle got there Marelda was rocking herself in Wilhelmina's rocker. Her hands were dead crabs resting on her apron. It was midafternoon and the window was open and a warm wind was blowing the curtains. Marelda's head was held cocked like a prairie falcon's listening for sound of danger.

The Turtle sat on the couch a few feet from her mother and waited out the silence. Then Marelda told her that she was the one who found the body. Wilhelmina had been sitting in her chair at her work-table. Marelda said she heard a thud and went to see. She saw her mother on the floor dying. Marelda spoke as she rocked herself and she gazed steadily at the floor. She went on, and her speaking was closer to chanting than to speech, saying that she went immediately to get Waldo who was outside working the garden and Waldo came running in and he got down and placed his ear to Wilhelmina's heart. Marelda meanwhile got the prayermeal and put a pinch on Wilhelmina's tongue. Then Lupe came running out of her room where she was making herself a new pair of moccasins for the fall ceremonies. Yolanda, who had just had her fifteenth birthday the day before, was out somewhere with a bunch of "bad" kids getting into trouble as usual. Marelda told the Turtle she sent Lupe to gather the women of the family.

At this point Lupe came in and came to her oldest sister and hugged her then the Turtle watched Lupe turn to meet the sternness in Marelda's face. The young girl sat down beside the Turtle and held her hands together between her bony, bony knees.

Painted Turtle listened to her mother tell Lupe to go to school and pick up the twins then Lupe jumped up and, saying she would be right back, dashed out.

Marelda repeated that she had sent Lupe to gather the women of the family and she added that some of the wives of Waldo's cousins came too. They gathered in Wilhelmina's room where they placed the body on the bed. A big wooden bucket of warm water made sudsy with the family yucca soap was brought in by Waldo's mother. Yolanda came home and was sent to the Council Headquarters to report the death. Marelda went on to say that she and Moira and Lavina and Lupe and Yolanda, when she came back, and the other women sprinkled the white prayermeal from their right hands and the black from their left. They then undressed Wilhelmina and scrubbed her entire body with the warm sudsy water. They used face-rags and Cannon towels. Then Marelda said she went to Wilhelmina's closet and selected her best black calico dress, one the young folks nowadays call an old squaw dress.

The Turtle closed her eyes, letting herself follow the chant. Marelda described how they stopped Wilhelmina's bottom hole with a corncob then put the dress on her. She heard her mother say that she and the other women knew for sure that Wilhelmina's death had been caused by a witch who lived down the road in a house facing the river just like their own. This witch, who was Wilhelmina's age, had envied Wilhelmina for years, ever since they were girls together long, long ago, back when most girls were well-behaved and never asked why they weren't initiated

84

like the boys. But the witch was jealous of Wilhelmina, especially of her success with jewelry, and finally got her magic to end Wilhelmina's life.

The litany rose and fell like that of some ancient representative of Achiyalatopa with the sword poised at the tip of his bottom lip. Marelda said when they finished dressing Wilhelmina's body in the dress of dignity and solemnity they sprinkled the prayermeal again around the bed and on the bed. Marelda herself took out from a locked drawer Wilhelmina's own private collection of jewelry she had made for herself over the years and decorated her wrists and fingers and ears and neck with them. Bedecked in turquoise and silver, Wilhelmina looked like a priestess ready to enter the glorious world of Kachina Village. After the dressing, one of the women brought the blanket. It was the best one in the house which happened to be a Navajo one Wilhelmina herself had traded a necklace and an inlaid set of earrings for. They placed the blanket on the bed and prayed over her body before rolling her over on it and wrapping her tightly in it.

Marelda talked on, in this singing voice, telling the Turtle these things with the unspoken understanding that she, as mother, knew that the listener, as daughter, needed to know them, having not been there; and there seemed to the Turtle a further understanding: the mother spoke with the assumption that the daughter had a debt to pay through the listening and the act too was punishment.

Marelda said she sent Lupe for the sewing kit and all the women worked at the task: some held the seams in place, others pushed the needles, threaded with strong cord, through the cloth, sewing Wilhelmina tightly into her warm, last earthly bedding. Marelda stopped. The Turtle listened to the curtains blown by the wind as they flapped gently against the window frame.

Marelda went on to say that while she and the women got Wilhelmina ready for burial, Waldo and his brother and a couple of his cousins and Albion and even the twins, helped to dig the grave. Marelda paused and the Turtle became aware that the radio was on back in the kitchen because the faint music ended and a man's voice said something about Joe Di Maggio hitting a home run that won a game somewhere. Marelda began to speak again, this time, keeping the chanting quality of her voice softer and lower. She said the menfolk dug but did not hit bone like so often and certainly did not unearth turquoise or silver as had happened occasionally in times past. Naturally they dug Wilhelmina's grave on the north side.

The Turtle felt both soothed and annoyed by her mother's chanting. Marelda said the family mourned for two days over the body then the men loaded it in the back of Waldo's pickup and drove over to the churchyard. Her grandmother was buried with her head pointing east so that she could be facing west with a view of Kachina Village over in Sacred Lake—as if it still was a place they could go—in Arizona. The Turtle stood and went to the window.

Then Lupe came in with the twins. Painted Turtle turned to see them standing there just inside the doorway. She could tell they didn't know who she was. Though only six they were the size of ten-year-olds. She held her arms open for them to come to her but they did not move.

86

Chapter 28
Indian Berry Soup

T his was the first time Peter Inkpen saw her play. He was out there in the noisy audience: a dinner crowd eating and drinking and laughing and not really watching and not really listening to this upstart Indian folksinger on the tiny, badly lit stage at Ranchito's. She had never heard of Inkpen and had no reason to know of or care about his presence. Now, as she always did when the crowd wasn't interested, she played for herself.

She sat on the edge of her chair. Her legs were crossed. Lately she'd crossed them because it felt more comfortable than doing it the old way. She lowered her head like a bird does to inspect the ground. The thumb of her left hand was behind the guitar's neck. She used only the tips of her fingers. Her right hand rested on the lower string. She was careful to keep her right elbow in close. Her knuckles were aligned with her strings. She was also careful not to touch her new guitar with her wrist. One foot rested on a footstool and the other on the floor. She fretted the strings, then plucked them, then fingered them. The lamb gut spoke of distance and the snow of ancient light. Her voice started up slowly, from a tone of meditation.

> Feed me Indian berry soup,
> Mother, feed me
> your campfire ribs

> for I am weary.
> Comfort me, Mother,
> with elk and crow.

She used her index finger to fret the first string then she used her middle to work the second one, single-string style. Her voice rose.

> Wrap me in your warm blanket,
> Mother. Feed me your good
> Indian berry soup!
> I hate myself, Mother.
> Carry me once more
> on your back
> in my little cradleboard.

Here, timing was crucial. She was playing evenly and keeping the melody coming slowly. No strums. She was getting a light, clear sound. Her voice was low and mournful. Some of the people stopped talking and began to listen.

> Tickle me, Mother.
> Feed me Indian berry soup.
> Tickle me with your porcupine
> quill, like you did
> when I was an infant
> on your back.

When she finished Peter Inkpen stood and clapped. This was unusual behavior in Ranchito's. Three or four others stood too, and joined the agent.

Painted Turtle looked for the first time at Peter Inkpen when he began clapping. She wondered who he was.

Chapter 29
Green Chile Stew

P eter came back the next night.

She was bent low, listening to her own music, having given up on the dinner crowd a half-hour after she started. This time she was aware of Peter Inkpen in the audience but she still didn't know who he was.

Bent low, she could hear her own strum better, listen better for the smooth, nicely subdued personality of her own bass. She'd worked hard at giving the bass more presence and now it was working. She followed it with a strong downstroke, careful with her pick, holding it gently on downstrokes. She used her index finger to get the right strum. She was in G. She listened to her runs and tags. She was ready to wed her voice to the effort of her fingers. The voice she heard lifting out of her body was solemn.

> The last Bow Priest died
> There will be no more
> but witches still turn
> into coyotes at night
> The last Bow Priest died
> There will be no more
> The witches peek
> in windows
> They claim drought

The last Bow Priest died
There will be no more
The witches say
they cause windstorms
can destroy our pueblo
The last Bow Priest died
There will be no more
The witches say they can
make a loved-one true
can cure heartache
The last Bow Priest died
There will be no more

She was singing softly but keeping the strings behind the words. She went through the words again. Her picking was flat. She changed the rhythm only slightly at the end. She went into C. Then G.

She went through the words once again. Before the final chorus she rushed the tempo, then broke in on G for the second time, stressing the word "last."

When she finished this one she saw that same man clapping again, then saw a few other people who stopped talking or eating and were clapping with him. The ovation went on for a few minutes. She felt as happy as Hank Williams on a good old night in Tennessee.

Again, she held her ear down to her instrument, taking the posture of a mother about to nurse an infant. She felt the audience recognize the loping tempo. There was a flutter of appreciation. That man's clapping, though, rang above the thud. She played with C for a moment, bending her wrist as far as she could for the proper effect. Lucky to have the forearm strength she had: all those years of hauling firewood in to the stoves and helping with the kneading of bread. Her fretting-hand was pressed firmly down. The tension felt so natural. The bow-and-arrow, she thought.

> I love my mother's green chile stew.
> To begin, she chops the lamb
> into cubes, using a long sharp knife.
> She dusts the pieces with flour
> and deep fries them in lard.

> I love my mother's green chile stew.
> As it cooks, she adds black pepper
> and crushed juniper berries, the chilis,
> dropping them into the black kettle.
> My sister adds the oregano.

> I love my mother's green chile stew.
> It cooks for two days,
> all of its ingredients simmering
> as I wait impatiently
> grinding corn.

They clapped and she thanked them and stepped down and the man who had clapped the loudest stood and came toward her, grinning, with a bottle of Budweiser in one hand and the other out-stretched, aimed at her like a rifle.

Chapter 30
Professional Quality

A t the top of the first intinerary Peter put together for her was a place she had already worked for free in Cuba, New Mexico called Blackbird Cantina.

She was pretty sure she was in Cuba again. She was trying to get to the cantina because she had to go on at eight. She came out of the bus station and a cowboy on horseback almost knocked her off the sidewalk, going by doing a sweep, rather trying to do one, but missed picking her up. The cowboy was singing like some kind of nut, "Tumbling Tumbleweeds," as he galloped by. When she saw that he was turning around—stopping traffic—intending to come back and try again, she ducked into a chili parlor and went to the women's room.

She looked at her wrist but there was no watch on it. The Blackbird was about five blocks down the main drag. She could not stay in the toilet forever so she came out. The coast was clear so she ran out and shot down the sidewalk.

She passed a cantina where somebody knocked on the window trying to get her attention. She glanced back over her shoulder. She saw a group she knew as The Andrews Sisters waving at her. She had seen them around and they worked some of the same joints she worked. They did a good imitation of the real Andrews Sisters. She waved back.

She kept running. She couldn't afford to be late for her first professional gig. She couldn't remember if she was supposed to follow a flamenco guitar player called Pablo Paz who had an uninhibited, highly charged style, who played Huelva and Paco il Barbero and El Maestro Patino and ranked himself with Carlos Montoya and Ramon Montoya and Nino Ricardo, or lead him, this mysterious Pablo Paz. At some other place—was it Ranchito's in Gallup, the Stardust Country Club in Phoenix, the Lazy L Motel's Lazy L Lounge in Albuquerque?—she had gone on after his act, a hard one to follow. While trying to play her quiet music and sing her quiet songs, his gypsy guitar kept ringing in her ears. She hoped this time she would lead.

The sun was going down when she threw herself against the swinging doors. A dude who called himself Tex Williams was on stage rehearsing with a group he'd put together called The New Spade Cooley Band. She went on through to the back looking for Tim the manager. Peter was supposed to have already contacted Tim. Somebody on a bar stool was trying to sing along with the guys rehearsing. He sounded like a dying dog.

She found fat Tim and he remembered her all right but he had heard nothing about her from Inkpen in Santa Fe. As the news sank in she felt foolish and almost wanted to go to the bar and just get drunk—a way she had never before wanted to be. Tim told her that Pablo Paz was going on at eight and good old Tex Williams and his New Spade Cooley Band would follow. Both acts were scheduled every night for a week. Then Tim wanted to know since when had she started booking through Inkpen. He remembered her passing around the hat.

Confused and hurt, she turned and ran.

In the cantina where The Andrews Sisters were drinking at the bar she ordered a dark beer. The girls knew her but she couldn't remember each of their names. One was called Maxine but the Turtle couldn't be sure which face to assign it to. After a noisy greeting scene, the one next to Painted Turtle wanted to know why she was in Cuba, where was she gigging. The Turtle chose not to lie. She told the part-singer what had just happened. This Maxine or Patti or Laverne wanted to know if the Turtle had given both her agent and the club boss a piece of her mind. She hadn't and she couldn't figure out why or how she could have. The part-singer thereupon began to lecture the Turtle on her ignorance, even accused her of not being in song-shape; gestured at her guitar and implied that her new guitar was cheap. The woman even went so far as to suggest to the Turtle that she was not of professional quality—having an agent like Inkpen and hoping to work a two-bit joint like the Blackbird. This was all the Turtle needed. She hit the ceiling.

She slapped the woman hard across the face and threw a dollar on the bar and walked out.

Chapter 31
Kyaklo

That night when she went to sleep in a tiny hotel room on the second floor of The Dollar and a Half Hotel, she knew there was a place she must go urgently but she couldn't remember—if she ever knew—how to get there. She saw herself—rather than feeling herself—searching along the edge of a lake, in a night without stars. She came to a village called Heshokta. She had heard the word before, perhaps from one of her grandparents. It was late and the village was still and dark. Somehow this seemed to be the place but she could not remember what she was supposed to do here. She walked into a narrow passage between two adobes; she went on, and before long she knew the village was based on the old rectangular plan of long, long ago; then she came to an adobe where there was a bright red ribbon tied to the top rung of the roof-ladder. She was sure the ribbon was a signal meant for her alone. Yet it did not bring back full memory of her urgent quest. Wasting no time, she climbed the ladder to the flat roof. Exhausted, she stretched out on her back to rest for a moment. Her heart beat like night rain against a window. Something in the air whispered in her ear. It said its name was Kyaklo. He told her he wished her no harm and although he knew he was not the reason she had come on this urgent mission and stopped on this roof, he nevertheless was

95

prepared to lend her some of his valuable time. She immediately told him that he could keep his time and even asked him to run along and tend to his own affairs. He smiled in the moonlight and she saw the great ugliness of his face and wanted to scream. But she did not. He then insisted that she was his affair—all the living beings were. He told her he wanted to escort her to Water's End. There she must give birth to twins and leave them to fate. It was too absurd. This was surely a dream, a stupid one at that! She told him she had already given birth to twins as a result of being raped and that the rapist's family had compensated by paying her father in sheep and jewelry and rugs and cash. He said that none of that mattered any longer, that he knew all about it and that what he had in mind was something of a revision of what had happened to her. He insisted that if she made the trip with him to Water's End she should no longer suffer the plight of a villain but would turn thereafter into the mother of heroic, even godly sons! She hesitated still. Meanwhile, she—and apparently he too—heard commotion down below. He said it was the sound of the less sympathetic ones coming, possibly to do her harm, to possess her or to beat her, or to do both. It would be unwise to wait another minute. Unable to decide what to do, she woke—in great urgency—and lay there in her narrow bed, cold, watching the neon lights of The Dollar and a Half Hotel flicking on the ceiling and on the wall.

Chapter 32
A Responsible Dream

Before long she was back at Zuni to see the boys and the folks but when she was ready to leave the councilmen sent word that she could not leave the reservation till she learned how to make the Sayatasha belt to perfection. In their message they told her that if she left without permission she would be picked up and would thereafter have to learn to do many, many other, more difficult things commonly expected of women.

So, she figured since she was here till she could plan a way to leave, she might just as well keep busy. With this thought in mind she took out the slopjars from all the sleeping rooms of the house; she ironed the shirts and the blouses she found in a pile on her mother's bed.

When she thought she had proven herself, the chiefs told her to learn to listen to the old stories. They were fetishes against bad luck and even death. They said she needed to cultivate the positive attitude of a humble sheep dog. She was not giving enough of herself to the family, the clan, the pueblo. The women said she made too much of having been raped.

They wouldn't let her leave. They told her to stay and encourage her sons to grow up to be good Zunis: to be modest and not ambitious. Teach them to respect grave-digging.

They told her to go out to Matsakya and tend to the turkeys. So

97

she found her way to Matsakya.

She sat on the turkey-yard fence singing a song.

> I live in Matsakya
> I tend the turkeys
> I talk with the turkeys
> They dress me up
> for the Yaaya Dance
> I promise them
> I will return
> before the fifth dance
> but I am having such fun
> I forget to stop dancing
> When I return
> my turkeys are gone

They told her let it be a lesson to her: it was just another example of her lack of responsibility.

But she deserved another chance because, well, she was of a good and respected family. They told her to be a good girl so often it was coming out of her ears. Chimiky ana kowa! She sang the song of herself as a girl.

> Call me makki
> When I was a girl
> I played hide and seek
> Once I hid in an ear of corn
> Nobody knew my corn-
> stalk, my silk
>
> Call me makki
> Inside, I met a corn-
> bore, Kesshe, he said
> This is my place and

> I said, No, this is
> my place: I hide here
>
> Call me makki
> Kesshe, I can shout
> in your face
> My shout scares
> little worms
> out of my corn

And hearing her sing this they told her it represented the right spirit and that she should practice what she preached.

When she had been behaving to their liking for a long while the councilmen told her she was free to go and come but they were sure now that she would rather stay. She left the minute they gave the word.

Chapter 33
The Song Trick

S he wanted to go back to see the boys but they wouldn't let her back on the reservation. They told her there was a certain document she needed which she was unable to present. And even if she had it it would be too late today because it was already after five and the new curfew went into effect every day at five. She showed them her guitar and a snapshot of the twins, one of her mother, her father, her recently deceased grandmother. They told her her effort was deceitful. She got mad and blew up in their faces. They told her to go fly a kite. They said they couldn't hear her. They told her to go to Blue Doors and play the slot machines. She told them she was born at the Middle Anthill and they had no right to keep her out. They told her her family was doing well and did not miss her. She showed them her old headband. They shook their heads and said it didn't matter. She told them she used to get up at five to help her mother bring in the firewood. It didn't mean anything now. When they had a goat, she fed it. When they had two hogs, she fed them. She went to sheep camp with her father. They told her to stick it in her ear. She said she cleaned ashes from the five stoves. She baked bread before she was ten. She cooked pancakes and fried the mutton. They told her she was wasting her time. She made cakes out of cornmeal. She sewed her father's and brother's longjohns. She sewed her own calico dresses and polished her black oxfords and pressed her manta and red belt and her sister's red checkered apron. She told them these activities meant she had been responsible. They wanted to know where was her proof. She said she'd sing them a song if they let her in. They thought about this, even put their heads together in conference. They told her she could try to get in this way but they couldn't promise her that her song would do the trick. She took the chewing gum out of her mouth.

> Once upon a time I ran
> away from home
> thought my folks mean
> They planted prayersticks
> against my family
> Moths flew around my head
> trying to seduce me
> to nest in my hair
> Exhausted and hungry
> I sat on a mesa
> I missed my family
> so I ran down to herders
> They hid me from moths
> but the moths found me
> so I ran from the camp
> back to my village
> and into my family's arms
> They removed the prayersticks
> planted against my family

The line guards told her her song was nice but that it wasn't good enough to get her back in. She called them dumb mudheads.

Chapter 34
A Hole in the Ground

Inkpen apologized for the mix-up. He booked her at Tim's Blackbird for a month later but, meanwhile, she gigged at the Stardust Country Club in Phoenix, the Lounge of the Lazy L Motel in Albuquerque, Club Ranchito's in Gallup, and maybe one or two other places. When she finished at Ranchito's, she had three days before she had to be back in Cuba.

She went to see the twins and the folks. Everybody was still sad about Grandma's death. It made her realize that the death was still swollen large inside herself too.

Seeking to be alone with her sons, she took them by the hands and went out and crossed the road to the old car on the riverbank. It now had no doors but the front seat was still sturdy enough to sit on although the springs were pushing up through the cloth. It was dusk. She sat in the middle. Dandelions were growing out of the dashboard. A couple of mustard sprouts were growing from sand packed by wind where the glove compartment once had been. A tiny mint sprout was holding forth above her head, embedded in dirt in the crease of the ceiling frame. Straight ahead, she saw the moon. It was snagged in the branches of the old cottonwood up the road. It had given up its struggle to free itself from the entanglement; like a he-dog stuck in a she-dog, it waited for the raging wind to die before freedom.

She asked them to tell her about Great Grandma Wilhelmina's death. You see, she wanted it from their point-of-view. Why? Because as an artist point-of-view meant a lot to her. Bryce said that Great Grandma died and she was now in a hole in the ground in the churchyard. Bruce then said that he and Bryce helped Uncle Albion and Grandpa Waldo dig the hole. He told her he had a little shovel and Bryce had a little shovel too. The dying came before the hole. Uncle Albion dug a lot at the hole. Grandpa Waldo dug too but he stopped to drink from his bottle. He kept taking it out of his back pocket just like he did when he worked in the garden. Then the councilman came out there when they had the hole dug. He told them it was in the wrong place. Bryce said they had to fill up the wrong hole and dig another hole in the right place. She asked them how far was the wrong hole from the right place. They both showed her by holding up their hands to measure the distance. When Bruce saw Bryce's stretch he made his larger. What else did the councilman say? He told Uncle Albion to dig the right hole. Yes, but what else? The councilman went over and took his shoe-toe and made an X where he wanted the right hole. Then what happened? They said they had had to fill up the wrong hole. When the councilman left, Grandpa took out his bottle again. After he drank he wiped his mouth with his sleeve. Uncle Albion dug and dug and they dug too. Bryce said he hurt his back. Bruce then said he too hurt his back digging. He said they dug the right hole deeper than the wrong one. When they finished digging they got down in the hole and it was cool down there. She wanted to know if anybody from the clan came out to perform the rituals. They didn't know what she meant. Then Bruce told her Grandpa drank his bottle-stuff then stomped around on the bottom of the hole. Bryce said it was a Ghost Dance Grandpa did. Bruce said Grandpa fell down. Uncle Albion said Grandpa was grace, said Bryce. Bruce said, No, Grandpa was a disgrace.

When she could no longer untangle herself from their confusing entanglement, she pulled them from the wreckage she still thought of as her summer home and started up across the road, headed back for the house.

Just as she started out with them she saw Old Larry Gchachu coming toward her. She felt her whole body grow rigid as he approached. He was walking slowly, with his cane as support more than sport. She remembered the fetishes carved into it and how fascinated she had been by it when she was a small girl. Nowadays, she had heard, he knocked things around with it, poked people, opened or shut doors with its tip, literally used it as a cruel instrument extended between himself and the rest of the world. It also, obviously, helped him walk.

Chapter 35
Stars and Planets

Seeing Old Gchachu, she told the boys to run along back up to the house. The minute she told them to do this she wondered why. It was as though she needed to get them into some sort of safety zone.

Old Gchachu spoke, saying kesshe and tosh iya and then went on to say that they had tried to call, semanawa, her in time. He paused and turned. She followed his gaze. They watched the boys run toward the house. They watched till the boys reached the house.

Old Gchachu then asked the Turtle to come down to the riverbank with him for the protection of the spirits that lived along the sacred river. She followed him.

He sat on a flat stone embedded in the sand.

She sat on the ground with her legs tucked under her, trying to imagine what he wanted to say to her. When had a woman ever been worth his time and attention? Half in English, half in Zuni, he began. It was not good.

He said he needed to talk to her. She expected as much. He then told her no society had much tolerance for diversity. When the Zuni boys came back from the second war they were different and had different ideas and the people laughed at them. The ones who didn't want to give up their new habits and be the way they were before going away had to leave. Nobody understood them anymore. She listened without watching his mouth or eyes. She, like he, was facing the river. It was the same with the women who chose to associate with the anglos—to smoke and drink. They can't stay here, can't keep their roots here, he said. Everybody would dislike them. This earth—he tapped it with his cane—was sacred: the sacred place of their ancestors. At this point the old man stopped and was silent for a moment before speaking again. Then he said that everything was in a sorry state nowadays. He gazed at the river. She looked at him doing this. He told her that Zunis who chose not to believe in the sacredness of this place had no business staying here. The young women of the race should want to replace the feeble old ones and those who die—and should feel honored to do so. There was no place for the diffident and the indifferent. She heard him say that the Zunis were the chosen people: the Ones-Who-First-Had-Being were their ancestors. They used the sacred prayermeal and planted prayersticks even in these untrusting times to try to protect themselves and to stay in the protection of the ancestors. He told her she had strayed from the protection of those old ways. He said he heard of her comings and goings and rumors of her doings.

Suddenly he threw his old white head back. His headband was bright red. Look! He pointed to the southwest. There was Towayalanne. When a Zuni got too far from Towayalanne his soul died. After death such a Zuni did not go to the Sacred Lake where Kachina Village was. He could not drink at the Sacred Spring. Such a Zuni died completely without rebirth. She was in danger of becoming such a Zuni. He said her father came to the kiva when she first started to wander and he and the other men prayed for her recovery. They asked the spirits of Halona to bring her back.

Then Old Gchachu was silent for a long while as he gazed with his discolored eyes at Corn Mountain. She watched him. He was thinking. You could see that. He began to speak again. He told her everybody knew it was no fault of her own that she had been raped as a child and worse—had had the bad luck to have twins. At least she had been raped by a Zuni and not a stranger and the Zuni had not been one of her own clan. The problem was she had not made the best of her lot in life. She wished he would stop repeating himself—or was he insisting on the point? He said she had gone off and cut herself off from her sons and her family and her clan, from the Zuni people. Had she stayed, a decent Zuni might have married her but now everybody knew about her shame and it was not likely that a Zuni of any type would want her even if she came back to stay. Perhaps some witchcraft had caused her downfall. He didn't know exactly who was behind it but he knew some evil was in the air. The shame she brought on her fine family might have also caused the death of her grandmother.

She looked away from his face at her own hands. She sat there beside him, waiting without knowing what she was waiting for. He was silent. She could hear his laborious breathing.

Using his cane as a support, he slowly stood and without saying farewell, slowly made his way back to the road.

She looked up at the scattering of stars and planets and knew that she would never understand anything as long as she lived.

Chapter 36
Electric Guitar

This is where I come in. My name is Baldwin Saiyataca. Close friends call me Baldy. The tone has to be right.

I met Painted Turtle in the Blackbird Cantina in Cuba during her opening night. As I told you earlier, Pete Inkpen—who was also my agent—had asked me to stop in and talk with her, to see if I could get her to jazz up her act. I play electric guitar. I've been through a lot of bands; formed two groups of my own. The one that lasted the longest and is still known—at least in the Southwest—was Raindance.

After her performance I bought her a drink. Because of some sort of infection she was drinking milk, so I bought her a glass of milk. She was really surprised to hear that Pete was also my agent. I lifted my guitar up from the floor so she could see my evidence. It was an Electra — one of the best you can lay your hands on. I got it real cheap.

I forget the name of the group that went on after the Turtle finished but they were pretty noisy so we decided to find another place to sit.

We ate enchiladas at a joint called Don Jose's, a couple of blocks down the main drag. I had a bottle of beer tilted toward my mouth when I asked her if she ever thought of playing electric. She waited till she finished chewing before she told me—in a flat voice—no. That no sounded so final I sort of made up my mind right then not to waste any more time on this effort on behalf of our agent. I frankly thought I'd like to make love to her so I decided not to risk making her mad by asking the wrong questions. Inkpen could round up his commercial stars elsewhere. This lady was special.

After the enchiladas I wanted to keep the night going but I sensed she was tired. I tried anyway. No, she wasn't interested in the belly dancer at Berino's Hideout; no, she did not want to gamble at a private club I knew in the back of Casa Machado; no, she didn't want to walk in the moonlight. She wasn't like other show folks I knew.

She said I could walk her to her hotel, which was a fleabag if ever I saw one. At the entrance, where a drunk was vomiting, she said goodnight and asked me to say hello to Pete.

I wanted to know if this was goodbye forever.

She told me it might not be. She said, you can never tell. Anything can happen.

Chapter 37
One-String-at-a-Time

T he next night I watched her perform again. She adjusted her instrument on her knee, resting it comfortably against her breasts. Her right hand was held delicately over the fingerboard with just the tips of her fingers touching the strings. She leaned forward into the light. Her thumb slid forward on the sixth string. She played it and the thumb rested on the fifth. The sound was good. She began.

I forget what she was singing.

Careful to avoid the raggedy sound that can result from the one-string-at-a-time style, she let each note have its own space and posture. Her fingers played the third and second strings then the first.

Then with the guitar she made the tingle-linging sounds of her horn-bells, using a free stroke. She came back to the refrain with the rest stroke which let her start again, faster.

I could see she felt the audience coming over into her rhythm, knowing the sunrise and the sadness of some kind of loss expressed in her music or the song or both. I went up on the highs and came down to the lows with her. She sang the words over and over and watched the entrance. I don't know why. At first I thought she was expecting somebody she knew. She played the guitar like it was a wheel of fortune.

Chapter 38
The Elevator

I was patient and we became lovers.

We left Cuba early in the morning and drove out of the way, reaching highway Ninety-five through the Navajo reservation because I wanted to go this way with her. It meant something special to me because of my father—and I wanted to share it with her. She was due to open again (by popular demand!) at Ranchito's in Gallup and that's where we were headed. I turned at One-ninety-one, going south, which is the best way through. The land was pink and lavender and the growing things were blazing green. Splashes of snow-white sandstone burst into sight before our eyes.

We reached Gallup and stopped at the first motel on Sixty-six with a vacancy sign. She told me she didn't think they let rooms to Indians. I said nonsense. She was reluctant to go in with me. I made her—I shouldn't have but I did. There was a middle-of-the-year feeling in my heart. The desk clerk pretended to busy himself with paperwork when we stepped into the office. I told him we wanted a room for the night—at least. He didn't look up from his nervous scratching. His voice shook when he told me there were no vacancies. There was no point in pushing him.

We drove farther down Sixty-six and stopped when we saw

another vacancy sign. It was the Amigo Motel.

We checked in. I didn't even mind the dingy sheets and the fact that we had to share the same towel. I was tired and happy to have a warm place to rest. We got in bed and I held her in my arms and looked up at the ceiling, then at the stupid wallpaper which was dark green with some dim design of murder and Mikado faces stuck in tulip buds.

I went to the toilet around three in the morning and discovered when I finished that it wouldn't flush. I've slept on dirt floors and used outhouses and wiped myself with leaves, but I never before felt so disgusted with myself and technology. I almost didn't go back to bed to sleep beside that beautiful woman because of the smell I had brought to our tiny room.

In the morning we moved to the Ocate Hotel on a side street up near the bus station. We knocked around all day that day, had a few drinks in a bar, ate hamburgers for supper, and turned in. I slept like a log.

When we came out of the elevator around ten headed for breakfast we saw a group of old Indians with two or three small children standing in the lobby facing the elevator. We went past. What were they watching—or waiting for? I looked back at the elevator door but saw nothing unusual about it. I asked the Turtle what she thought but she had no idea.

After a breakfast of greasy eggs and bacon and fries we went back and the Indians were still there. I went over to the desk clerk and asked what was going on. Meanwhile, I gave him money for another night. While the clerk was getting my change and—I guess—trying to formulate an answer to my question, I turned and looked again at the Indians. Painted Turtle came to my side. The men were wearing dusty, sweat-stained cowboy hats and old wool suits which were dirty and creaseless and the

112

women were dressed in shapeless black squaw dresses and wore black shawls over their heads. The children were barefoot. They were Navajo. I didn't know them as individuals but I knew them as my father's people. I was concerned.

As the clerk counted out my change he told me that the Indians were watching the elevator. I said I could see that. He laughed. An anglo came in through the front door. The clerk told me to watch the man. Painted Turtle and I followed his movement. He went directly to the elevator. The anglo pushed the up button and stood waiting for the contraption to come down.

I glanced again at the Indians: they were dead serious and hadn't blinked an eyelid.

The clerk then told us to watch closely. The elevator came to rest on the lobby floor. The door opened and the anglo got in and the door closed. Simple.

We waited while the Indians watched.

A minute or two later the elevator door opened again and a woman and two children walked out into the lobby.

The clerk was grinning when we looked at him. He wanted to know if we got the idea.

I looked again at the group of Indians. They calmly turned their heads, watching the progress of the woman and the two children across the lobby. You couldn't tell by their expressions how amazed they were. I thought of my father. I wondered about myself.

Chapter 39
The Zuni Sacred Lake

We were going southwest after the sun came up; out of Gallup on Forty and just before Sixty-one I noticed that the Turtle was intently watching the roadside as though she hadn't seen it before. I wondered what was on her mind. My impression was she had slept well in the night and was therefore rested. The week at Ranchito's had gone well, I thought. I had passed up an opportunity to gig at La Paloma in Valencia with a group called Hot Fudge just to stay with her. It was a great morning and I couldn't help expressing it. I started singing as I drove. I forget what I bellowed out but, boy, I was going at it some when she turned to me and asked me in this cool voice to pipe down.

Pretty soon I found out what she had in mind. She wanted to take a detour—but at first she didn't tell me why. Just do it was her command. Well, you can imagine: I got pissed. But I turned where she told me to turn; if she wanted Sixty-one—Sixty-one it was! I controlled my anger pretty well.

After five or six minutes of driving on Sixty-one (and my Bug was taking the road pretty well) I asked her if she minded telling me where we were going. This was a pretty indirect route to Phoenix, where she was due to open at the Stardust Country Club in two days. She took her time about answering. I said to myself: Well, well. And that's when xyz hit the fan. She accused me of having things my way all the time. I questioned the soundness of her accusation. She got a tight lip and sat focused on the gullies and scrubgrass and stunted trees.

I refused to give in to grim silence. I have a tendency to do that. In five more minutes her stubbornness dissolved and she told me she wanted to find the Zuni sacred water—called Spirit Lake. I had heard about it and read about the legal problems in the *Navajo Times*. Back when she was a small girl, she told me, boys were allowed to go over there with the men—their fathers and uncles—to bring back buckets of white clay which was used as ceremonial paint. She had always wanted to go with them but was never allowed. They went over every other year or every third year. The stories she heard about the trip over grew large in her mind and stayed with her as she grew older. Worse, when her own sons had not been initiated, she knew they too would never get to go. And now, maybe nobody—not even the most sacred members of the most respected kivas—would ever be able to go again. There was some sort of legal problem. The damned lake was way the hell here in Arizona, for god's sake! But I was patient and I understood her interest. I wasn't born at Tewa to a Hopi mother for nothing. Somebody planned it that way and also planned my reaction.

We drove into Saint Johns within twenty minutes. It boasted being Arizona's most livable little city. I pulled into the first gas station I saw. I stuck my head out the window and saw the boy coming. He had a big friendly smile and a "How you folks doing" all over his face.

I got out and stood by the kid as he filled it up. He asked if we were from around here and I said Gallup. The Turtle leaned across the seat and called me to the window. In a hushed voice, Painted Turtle asked me to ask the attendant if he could tell us

115

how to get to the Zuni Sacred Lake. Immediately, I was aware of the irony of the situation: a couple of Indians asking an anglo for the location of an Indian sacred place. I wasn't sure I wanted to place myself so squarely in such an absurd position. But I hesitated only a moment. For her I shot the question. As you might guess, the kid didn't know what I was talking about.

I paid him and we drove away, back onto the main road, moving slowly till we came to One-eighty—which would take us into Hunt. She had heard that the sacred lake was near Hunt or in Hunt. Or was it between Hunt and Saint Johns? The Turtle said she knew this much from gossip and maps and legend and newspaper articles dealing with the legal question of ownership.

I drove us slowly on to Hunt. The Turtle frantically watched not only her side of the road for sign of water but mine as well—despite our agreement that I would keep an eye on the driver's side and she, her own. We were trying to spot the Little Colorado or the Zuni River. Spirit Lake was supposed to be at the intersection of the two. That was one theory. So far, no markings.

The morning was losing its freshness. Something, not exactly weather, was oppressive out here and it was everywhere in the air. We hadn't felt any of this coming down. Up ahead was the curve for Concho. She asked me to slow down. Her body grew tense with excitement.

She told me to stop the car.

I stopped the car.

She sniffed the air then got out and inhaled it deeply. She darted about the road, sniffing with her nose turned up like a bear trying to catch a scent of berries on the air. I sat there at the wheel, bewildered, watching her. She had worked her way off the pavement into the grass, still sniffing, knocking the tall grass aside. Had she lost her mind? Then she came running back to the car.

She was sure, she said, that the sacred lake was somewhere in this area. She could smell it. She also sensed it in some other—perhaps mystical—way. I made an effort to be patient.

I got out and looked around. I saw nothing but dry land: red and white clay with weeds and cacti growing from it. If there was excessive moisture in the air I wasn't catching it in my nose. Then we heard a thudding sound. It was definitely the sound of some sort of machinery, perhaps a motor.

We saw, coming down the road toward us, a farmer on a tractor. It took him quite a while to reach us. His tractor was a John Deere and it was bright green and clean as a new bonnet.

When he reached us he thought we were just admiring the morning and the countryside and broke into song about the beautiful sky and the nice little flowers. What a pleasant man, I thought. He raised a hand toward the mountains in the distance and declared them holy enough to calm any man's soul. Speaking of that which is holy, said the Turtle to the farmer, did he have any idea where the Zuni Sacred Lake was located. The farmer scratched his chin and scowled. He turned his motor off because we had been talking to him and he to us above the hum, and now he spoke in a normal voice. He never heard of a Zuni sacred lake around these parts. Then he took it back and said, unless she meant that old place everybody called Stinking Springs. The farmer stammered then went on to say that Stinking Springs was a local joke. Some folks thought it just about the nastiest place on earth it smelled so bad. It was just an old mudhole cows wouldn't even drink out of anymore. Stinking Springs was kinda strangely situated: most of it was running through the private property of Seven Springs Ranch. He always had trouble remembering the name of the folks who owned the ranch. Other parts of Stinking

117

Springs and its drainage, he said, were on the lands of two or three other families. He paused to cackle a bit, enjoying his own memory of something funny. One joke had it that the place stank so because so many dead bodies were rotting in it and had been down there rotting for centuries, possibly millions of years. Apache—and this was Apache County—didn't want those stinking waters any more than anybody else, he told us. He wasn't speaking meanly. He perhaps wasn't even aware that we were offended. I glanced at Painted Turtle. I could tell by the squint of her eyes that she was furious with this innocent man on his shiny tractor. The Zuni Sacred Lake, if you are Zuni, is not a laughing matter.

Giving our "friend" the farmer the benefit of the doubt, I thanked him and said goodbye.

We drove on. I felt—I'm not sure how I felt. Perhaps I felt disillusioned; but I had had no illusions to begin with, except for those I had acquired through my empathy with the Turtle. The road was straight like a ceremonial sash laid out across a table with a red slice—the road itself—through the green on both sides. As we drove on toward Hunt I think we both knew, without saying a word, that Spirit Lake was behind us and in front of us and above us and below us and all around us, from the beginning of time and would be till the end of time.

I looked at the Turtle and she was crying but she soon dried her tears and gave me one of her great smiles.

The silver-green roadside shrubbery was brilliant in the morning light.

We passed through Hunt before we knew it.

118

Chapter 40
One Rose

We reached Phoenix just before midnight. The Turtle was
complaining about her sinuses and abdominal cramps.
We were hungry and the town seemed closed down. In the car we
had only a half bag of potato chips between us. We drove around
till we spotted a late-night soda pop and newspaper store. I went
in and bought a box of powdered doughnuts and a carton of milk.
Back in the car, I gave the bag to the Turtle.

Then we drove to the Trail Dust Motel down at the
southeastern end of town, the only place I knew that was cheap
and not hesitant about Indians. The desk clerk was the owner.
He was an anglo with a glass eye and a long bald head and a
strange accent. Maybe he came from some place like Finland. I
asked him to wake us at eight.

In the room we ate the doughnuts and drank the cold milk and
went to bed, curled up together to keep warm, and at eight sharp
the next morning I heard the owner knock at the cabin door. I
called out thanks and listened to him walk away. Meanwhile, the
Turtle crawled into my arms and began telling me her dream. In
the night her Grandma Wilhelmina was alive. She'd been accused
of witchcraft because a man named Frank Smith, a Zuni arrow-
maker, died. Everybody knew she thought old Smith was a pain-
in-the-you-know-what with his love for her. Old Gchachu took

119

Wilhelmina into the old church and pointed up at the beams. There was no roof so you could see them black and huge against the blue sky. The Turtle was somehow only a detached witness to the two figures standing on the dirt floor of the old church. But the Turtle was aware that Grandma Wilhelmina was already dead. In reality, the Turtle told me, Smith never had any romantic interest in her grandmother.

We made love, then washed ourselves at the face bowl, then went out to find a restaurant. Just as we reached a little shopping plaza I caught sight of my old drunk Aunt Franny, a Hopi outcast who'd been drifting around Phoenix, living with a small band of Hopis, for about twenty years. I ducked and kept my head turned, trying not to be seen. No, actually, I tried to hide myself behind the Turtle but I was too big and Aunt Franny's old eye too sharp. I heard her calling, Baldy! Baldy!, and I had to fake surprise when I turned in response. Well, you can imagine what happened. Smelly old Aunt Franny wanted to have breakfast with us. This was a bit unusual because nobody ever saw her actually eat. My mother Ruth always said Aunt Franny drank her breakfast and drank her lunch and drank her dinner. The wonder was she apppeared healthy and her mind wasn't a rotten piece of fruit. She talked with good sense the few times I saw her on the streets of Phoenix.

We found a greasy-spoon—the only place in sight—and took a table by the window and ordered bacon and eggs. Outside the window an old Mexican man was sitting on one of the park benches forming a little square under a big tree. He looked dead. He might have been. The wind hadn't been strong enough to blow him over. As we waited for food, I absentmindedly answered my aunt's questions about Ruth and Mike and other folks she knew at Tewa Village. A fancy French car came down into the sunken plaza area, circled and stopped in front of an Indian jewelry shop. The food came, brought by a Mexican woman wearing a plastic yellow apron. A little girl with a huge gap between her front teeth brought the toast on a platter bigger than her head. The woman poured coffee into our cups. A film of grease moved around on the surface when I stirred sugar into it. It was hard to know what to say to Aunt Franny. She was mumbling to herself and hadn't looked once at Painted Turtle since we sat in the booth. I thought about my aunt's eyes. I asked her how they were. She told us the Eyes story. I had heard it many times before. To make a long story short, her eyesight was bad. Then we got the Back story. I knew that one too. But at least she was talking. My aunt took a half-empty pint bottle of Jack Daniels from her purse and poured about two ounces into her coffee. She said it was her medicine. Doctor's orders. She cackled and the cackle caused rumbling in her lungs. She put the bottle back.

I was facing her and the Turtle. I could see the discomfort in my friend's face. Suddenly my aunt turned to Painted Turtle and said, "Do you know he's ashamed of me? They all are." And without waiting for a response, she concentrated on picking up her cup. It was hot so she was careful. I watched her hold it with both hands, move it slowly to her mouth and press it to her bottom lip. She made her mouth into a fistula through which she blew at the hot liquid. She sat her cup down after one sip and cackled again. We weren't let in on the humor. By now the Turtle had picked up her fork and was attempting to saw off a bite-size piece of fried egg. I bit into a slice of toast. Aunt Franny mumbled, apparently to Painted Turtle, that she was my mother's oldest sister. Her posture was that of someone waiting for a stoplight to change. "They don't allow me back on the reservation, you know. He can tell you. It's 'cause I married outside, married an anglo."

121

Aunt Franny was right. Despite myself—my desire to be open-minded—I felt ashamed that she was my aunt and especially bad that the Turtle was meeting her. The Turtle was chewing egg. I chewed toast. My aunt took up her cup again. Her eggs were no doubt getting cold. I closed my eyes and chewed the buttered bread. I didn't want to think. I didn't want a memory. My Aunt Franny had once crapped in her pants while standing on a roof watching a ceremonial dance. I wanted my memory to go away for a while. My Aunt Franny was supposed to be rich but stingy. I didn't believe it. You can count the rich Indians on the fingers of one hand.

The door opened and a little Mexican boy with a basket of roses came in. He came over to us. We were the only customers. Meekly, he gestured toward the roses without saying anything. I was about to send him away when I noticed my aunt digging in her purse. She came up with a change purse; she extracted a quarter from it and pressed the silver thing into the boy's dirty palm. With the other hand, which had an old scar on the back, he gave her one rose. I watched her grin at the boy. Her teeth were green around the gums.

My aunt turned to Painted Turtle and told her to hold still, then she stuck the stem of the rose into the Turtle's hair. It looked pretty there on the side of her head. Yet I felt humiliated, somehow. Still, the Turtle looked pretty damned good with the rose so brightly and sharply contrasted against her silky black hair.

I don't remember much about what happened after the rose, probably not much. I doubt if any of us finished our eggs and bacon. Maybe I drank my coffee; I'm sure my aunt finished hers.

Chapter 41
Belly-up

Nobody's ever heard of Limbo, New Mexico—it's so tiny you can hold your breath and walk from one end down the main drag to the other. It's on the border between New Mexico, Arizona, Utah, and Colorado. They call it Limbo, New Mexico officially only because Arizona, Utah, and Colorado are nice states and do not choose to fight over the possession of this postage-stamp of a town. They have bigger and better things to squabble over. Limbo was the next town the Turtle was scheduled to open in.

So we drove straight north, up past the Grand Canyon, and spent most of the day doing that, taking our time, and got into Limbo before sundown. It's the only way you're likely to get a room, even in a fleabag. The sun was squatting on the mountain range to the west and the desert to the right was turning a cool yellow-white. In most ways it was just another dusty little western town with all the usual bad luck you come to expect such a town to have.

We checked into the Lazy Palm Motel. We washed up and went out to the patio. By now it was dark and they had the electric lights on. A few people were lounging in chairs. A man wearing a big sombrero was walking around the area and clearly soliciting contestants for something that was about to happen.

You could tell because most were responding with a mixture of embarrassment and delight at what he proposed. When he got to us we got the drift. A limbo contest was about to start. The Turtle clapped her hands and squeaked like some exotic bird. I couldn't believe it. She was acting like a schoolgirl. It was very un-Zuni behavior on the part of a grown woman. It took a minute or two for her outburst to attract me, but in the end I liked it on her.

A big fat Mexican guy tried it first and fell on his butt before he bent back two inches. Everybody laughed.

We moved in closer to see the action. A teenage girl tried it and did pretty well but knocked the pole down on her third try.

The man in the sombrero was urging each constestant on, baiting them with the prize, which was some sort of huge toy—a teddy bear, I think. Two chubby women tried it together and flunked right away. A thin, drunk man—still holding his tall glass of whatever with a cherry in it—got so tickled by his own efforts he couldn't get started for his own and the crowd's merriment.

The Turtle's turn came. I held my breath. She got under the first four or five levels without trouble, then you could see she was bending backward with great effort. The people urged her on. She'd gone farther than anybody. Chances were nobody on earth could get under the bottom level. It was maybe eight, maybe ten inches from the pavement. A military jet went by overhead. We all grew silent for a moment. The Turtle, too—although she was bent halfway under the pole. When the tremor passed, and somebody laughed and spoke, we all, I think, cheered up again.

I imagined the Turtle felt removed from the pain in her back, watching herself doing this. Why was she doing it? Surely she didn't want the stupid toy. I was discovering another dimension to the Turtle's personality. But what good would it do me? I was in love with her. Enough of that! I saw the pain moving around in-

124

side her like a restless windswept fire.

She was an ancient goddess suspended between life and death, in eternal postponement. Yes, I knew Kafka, and I didn't discover him at Tewa. Painted Turtle was learning how dangerous arms were. They rested nowhere comfortably but helped balance—when all things were equal.

I, like the crowd, continued to hold my breath the lower she got. And she got very, very low. I had no idea she was in shape to do such a thing! You can imagine my surprise! You could tell she smelled her own sweat and saw double. Tears ran down her cheeks, ran into her ears, down her neck. I tried to catch her eye at the most crucial moment, but it was impossible. She braced herself against the pain and took two tiny, miserable puffin-steps under the pole and without knowing it, her face cleared it. When she opened her eyes and didn't see the pole above her, she relaxed, dead-still, flat on her back, resting. Everybody clapped for a godawful time.

The man in the sombrero led the clapping and shouted above the din that the lady was the winner.

The Turtle finally got up and took a bow. The teddy bear was then thrust into her arms but she seemed embarrassed. I felt for her.

The next night she opened at Club Limbo. The place was a dream with a nightclub room inside it. The customers were made of wood and cloth, they moved stiffly like dolls. Painted Turtle sang as she moved among them.

> I danced around the Zuni jug
> a flying jib
> There's a song in me
> the rapist destroyed

125

> I danced around the Zuni jug
> trying to find that song

She cast a spell. She turned herself into Citsuka—a black figure behind a white facade. When she struck her guitar strings, lightning flared out in different colors. The customers were amazed by the zigzags.

> Citsuka, I play you
> my lamb-gut music
> Citsuka, my wounds
> are not flat, I play
> straight, one-at-a-time
> notes with two tones
> Citsuka, I play you

I was caught in her spell. She strolled around the darkened room, between the tables on which candles flickered from the coming of her power. On her chest was the circular design of the hepakine. She spoke in the voice of Salimopiya.

She went back to the stage and sat on the edge of the stool and changed herself into Kwelele.

> Kwelele, your absent-soul
> takes charge of me
> Kwelele, I am suspended
> at the bottom
> of your shadow, inside
> your light
> Kwelele, your absent-soul
> is passionate
> while mine is passive

I felt her rhythm tingle my spine—I felt the tingle from the bottoms of my feet to the roots of my hair. She moved faster. She

showed the customers a corncob—held it between her legs, waved
it from side to side. The customers laughed.

> Koyemci, are you Wantateu
> or Awanpekwin
> or Posuki or Nalaci?
> Koyemci, did you plant
> the seeds for the crops
> and create your own soul
> from the footprints
> I left in your dust?
> Koyemci, lift your kilt
> and show us your lack
> of lust, your limpness
> Koyemci, I sing
> your innocence, I dance
> your blessing

Having finished singing this song, she began to move restlessly
back and forth across the little stage. She was a black figure
decorated with snowflakes, trying to seduce winter. She told the
customers that some of her spots were yellow, others red—not all
of them white. She had two voices.

> How do you, Calawitsi,
> get your spots?
> From the red corn
> from the juice
> of a secret plant
> Why do you not come
> naked as in the past?
> Because my people
> changed to shame
> So I cover myself

Then she went off stage, carrying her guitar like a batch of geese and jackrabbits flung over her back. I didn't know if anybody else could see them but I saw in her right hand a stick of black wood and in her left, the cedar bark.

Chapter 42
Her Lover

W hen I called Inkpen to see what was lined up for me all he wanted to know was how I was doing in my effort to transform Painted Turtle into a commercial property. I gave him some sort of offhanded answer. I asked again about work. He told me there was nothing for me. I hung up and went back to the room.

We checked out at eleven and headed for Bombay, New Mexico. I'd never been there but had heard that people could be seen on the streets in red pants and white shoes and old ladies walked about clutching poodles. Banditos lurked in the hills just outside of town. It was the end of April and the hottest day on record and my Bug had no air conditioner. Bombay was actually not in New Mexico—it only seemed to be. It was just north of Limbo, at the foot of Anasazi ruins which were not well-known like those at Canyon de Chelly.

I had misgivings about going to Bombay. Exactly why I felt so uneasy remained a mystery to me too long.

In any case, it took us ten minutes to size up the town. We walked proudly into the lobby of Maharashtia Hotel. It looked like it had been nailed up with No Trespassing signs all over it since the Mexican-American War and just recently opened for business without having been repaired or even dusted. A legless

Indian sat on the floor just inside the door with his hand held out. Over a door at the end was painted the word *Bar*. The Turtle would open there that very night. We should have turned and walked out right then.

Later, we went out and walked through the open market. This wasn't the end of the world but you could see it from here. We browsed among the Arabian-Mexican junk: spices, peppers, baskets, sandals, fetishes, pots, blankets, masks. We strolled among Sikhs and Hindus with serious faces. The music for snake charmers drifted from some back street as we crossed the plaza in front of a cantina where the jukebox was whipping out the sounds of a mariachi band.

Painted Turtle always told me her voice was as much a part of her body as her hands or feet, but that night, while singing in the Ayya Dining Room, she felt removed from her own voice. Even so the separated voice seemed to have taken good care of itself because the performance was one of her best. She was spared the cheerfulness of its brash company. But the sense of her rode on its words.

> I am Shumeekuli
> My name is Shumeekuli
> My face is black
> My face is flat
> I cure the insane
> I am the insane
>
> I am Shumeekuli
> My name is Shumeekuli
> My face is blue
> My face is yellow
> I dance far inside
> the Horned One's circles

I am Shumeekuli
My name is Shumeekuli
I dance the Yaaya
This is not a mask
This is my own face
I come from the lake

The audience clapped like people trying to smash flies in midair. I loved the distance I felt from them.

When the Turtle finished that night and we were having dinner at a corner table, a dark-complexioned man about my own age came over and introduced himself as Mister Andalusia. He wore long sideburns and had a dimple in his chin. His bowtie was black. He complimented Painted Turtle's singing profusely, then after I asked him to sit down and join us, he bluntly told her he wanted to paint her toenails. The Turtle and I looked at each other and laughed. Mister Andalusia didn't crack a smile. He sat with his fingers locked together on the table, like a good and proper fifth grade student. The Turtle, of course, didn't know what to say, and seeing this, Mister Andalusia spoke up. He suggested that she give his request some thought. But for now, would it be all right for him to join us for dinner. I reluctantly gave him a positive sign.

A West Indies calypso band was on the stage now playing island music. The sound was brassy and tinny. Mister Andalusia's tostadas were brought by a sullen waiter who nearly dropped the things in his lap. The Turtle was picking gingerly at some curry dish. I don't remember what I had. I do remember that I hardly ate it after the toenail-painter joined us. The three of us finished off the meal with some sort of cinnamon and coconut dessert which, the head waiter said, originated in Ceylon.

I was thankful when dinner ended and we were able to say

goodnight to Mister Andalusia.

Now, at this point we must return to reliance on my imagination. At dawn the Turtle got up and dressed. I was still asleep. She felt driven by an irresistible force. She whispered something to me just to test the level of my sleep. I didn't respond. She then tiptoed over to the door and let herself out and quietly closed the door. When she stepped outside, she saw a black Cadillac limousine parked alongside the Bug. A uniformed chauffeur was at the wheel. She looked closely. Behind him in the passenger seat was Mister Andalusia. He was intently watching her with a half-smile.

The chauffeur got out and held the rear door open for her; she climbed in beside Mister Andalusia. Not a word passed between them. The chauffeur returned to the driver's seat and started the engine. It purred like a happy house cat.

On the highway the car moved at a hundred miles an hour till they came to a dirt road without a sign. Here, the driver turned off and drove somewhat slower till they reached a blue lake hidden by a tall stand of evergreen—spruce, firs and pine. The car stopped here.

The chauffeur opened the door for them and they got out. Mister Andalusia offered her his hand and she took it. Together they walked to the edge of the water. She looked down into it. It was so clear she could see the bottom. She glanced across to the other side. This was the most beautiful lake she had ever seen. There were not the usual lake-smells of wren-droppings and cod and no evidence of abadejo flies. Already, this early, the sun was pouring down so that she pulled her magenta-colored shawl over her head and she removed her other hand from that of the strange man beside her. Nearby, sunken into the earth, was a large boulder. Her mind was arid, her mood desolate.

She left the man and went to the boulder and straddled it. She sat there swinging her feet. Her shoes fell to the ground. She kept swinging. She was a Maya goddess and the lake before her was her mind. No, she was not Maya. She was simply a Zuni girl. She was waiting for the appearance of her secret lover from a forbidden tribe. He would come to court her any moment. He would be a Kassa in black and white makeup wearing corn beads. His hair would be tied in two horns. Her father would flog the boy with cornhusks.

From the boulder she saw human movement in the underbrush of milkweed and wild onion growth on the other side of the lake. Or had it been an animal—a bear? She glanced at Mister Andalusia. He seemed in a trance as he gazed at the surface of the water. She looked over her shoulder. The chauffeur was at the wheel reading a newspaper.

Mister Andalusia then went to her but just before he was within touching distance she held her hand out the way a traffic cop does to stop an approaching car. Then, as though she were in some sort of opera, she sang to him.

> My lover is a Cane Chief
> My lover is a Medicine Society Chief
> My lover is a Grasshopper Chief
> My lover is a Shichu Chief
> My lover is Chief of Corn of All Colors
> My lover carries the Cross
> He dances the burro kachina dance
> He shears his father's sheep
> He wears a Kumeoishi mask
> He wears a Chakwena mask
> He wears sumkup
> He decorates the Kekei Virken
> He whips the invisible woman
> He purifies through beating her

He kneels before Saint Augustine
He makes an offering to the Old Man
My lover plants prayersticks
My lover wins in the footrace
My lover is the Town Chief
My lover dances the Soyal
My lover plays the Butterfly Boy
My lover is called Polhiktiyo
My lover blesses my home
He plants seeds
He chews the root ballafia
He feeds me piki
He is the Mapurnin
He makes mudcakes
He wraps them in cornshucks
My lover is Chu, Snake-dancer

Mister Andalusia was firmly held off by the intensity of the song. He wasn't going to be able to move till she let him. He was like winter waiting for a warm fall to end.

But her song ended and he came close enough to touch her rock. And he did. He stroked its surface. "Buenos dias, Senorita Etawa!" He spoke as though he had just arrived. She returned his greeting in a language she wasn't quite sure she knew. She leaned down toward him and plucked his gold sash. She then took the gold cigarette holder with its burning cigarette from between his fingers and took a puff, then handed it back. She knew without looking that the chauffeur was watching.

She sat up straight and continued to swing her feet. Suddenly he grabbed the nearest one and kissed the big toe. Its nail instantly turned red. He kissed each toe and following each kiss, each nail turned red. She smelled nail polish. She looked at Mister Andalusia's lips. They were red as a fire engine. He managed to do this painting so quickly she hardly had time to stop him. She had momentarily lost control of herself. He had gotten her foot before she knew it. But now she was determined he would not get the other one. Besides, he had to move to the other side of the boulder to do that. In the meantime, she could put him—again—in his place. The largest part of her spirit wanted to do this.

> My lover lives on First Mesa
> My lover gazes at Corn Rocks
> My lover watches the curve of Mishongnovi
> My lover dreams of Chimopovi
> My lover drifts through Keams Canyon
> He dances in his overalls
> He wears a Stetson hat and jeans
> My lover at tungwayane was named Dog Face
> My lover grew up doing the Home Dance
> My lover smokes yellow pine handrolled
> My lover kills the eagle
> My lover tells the story of the Ragweed Girls
> My lover fucks the Ragweed Girls to death
> My lover eats midget corn and lamb stew
> My lover eats his mother's frybread
> My lover attended government school
> He wore government shoes
> He brushed his teeth at school
> He grew up in an eagle's nest high on a rock
> My lover helped his father work
> My lover's people stayed to themselves
> My lover lives no longer at First Mesa
> My lover lives inside the words of my body

Meanwhile, Mister Andalusia was beating his way through the weeds, trying to get to the other foot. She kicked him.

He fell in the wet grass.

Meanwhile, back at the motel, as he fell, I woke up.

135

Chapter 43
Your Place

I was wide awake, and determined now to stay on course. The Turtle and I had places to go to. I hardly cared anymore about Inkpen's plans for me. I was in love with a great artist, a poet, a beautiful person. She was giving me a new reason to want to live. Before I met her I had thought seriously of killing myself—life was so unpromising, so full of disappointment. Now travelling with the Turtle, I was open to the magic of May. Tijuana, Colorado? Yes, it was a real place. It was our next stop. She was supposed to open at the Ole Cantina there in two days—and, wouldn't you know it, the place was damned smack in the middle of the Red Light District.

This tiny town was near Santa Fe—you wouldn't even have believed it was in the state of Colorado because of the roadmaps that tell you otherwise. Tijuana! What a magical name!

We found the Ole Cantina pretty quickly. We then decided not to seek out the owner till we had a chance to check out the joint. It was noisy and upbeat all right. There were a whole bunch of scientists in there getting drunk. One cowpoke at the bar told me they were from the atomic energy installation twenty-two miles outside of town. I bought the cowpoke a drink. When he finished it and I wouldn't buy another one, he wandered off. The Turtle elbowed me in the ribs. I looked where she was looking. Some heavily painted putas who had just picked up a bunch of half-drunk hombres were escorting them out of the bar. A hotel was upstairs. I sipped my scotch. I asked the Turtle how was the white wine. She held the glass to my mouth. I took a sip. Yup, it was from a Mexican grape all right. Down the bar some charros with their weekend pay were raising hell. One escaramuza wearing a ten-gallon hat was arguing with a fake matador about a loose plank in some fake bullring that had caused a friend of hers to get injured by a fake but vicious bull. I heard the escaramuza tell the matador that she did the best rayos of all the cowgirls. Her back was to me but I could see his face when I looked out the sides of my eyes. The escaramuza told the matador that her horse was the best in all southern Colorado and northern New Mexico and northeastern Arizona and northwestern Oklahoma and southwestern Kansas. You should have seen his face. If she hadn't been a woman he would have punched her in the nose. I felt the Turtle's elbow again. I followed the line of her gaze. Two Mexican girls in adelinas had just come in and were standing by the door with their hands on their hips. All this was happening to the jukebox music of a mariachi band.

The mariachi ended and a salsa started. It was sort of jazzy. Pretty awful. The sound caused me to almost bite my glass. I finished the scotch and ordered a margarita. The escaramuza stopped talking to the matador and started watching the girls by the door. She said in Spanish that they really thought they were something but she knew they were tramps pretending to be respectable.

When I finished the margarita and caught the bartender's attention to get another one, he looked like a man who had swallowed something he knew he should have left on his plate. I changed my mind and cancelled when the Turtle asked me if I was sure I needed it. I knew finally that the revised decision was the best one when I almost fell in attempting to turn to search for the men's room.

That was our introduction to the Ole Cantina and a sampling of some of the people of the area. Two nights later the place was hardly any different, except that they lowered the lights and unplugged the jukebox and aimed a light on Painted Turtle who stood at the back of the room on a table the boss and the bartender had rigged up to look like a stage. Even after she struck the strings of her guitar and played a warm-up chorus, the crowd kept right on in its noisy way as though she were a jukebox or less.

> There are ways to speak of
> the scarecrow in the cornfield
> the taste of paperbread
> the souls of one's ancestors
> the corrals of one's sheep camp
> the drying of fruit and pepper
> ways to speak of your place
> > in it all

> There are ways to speak of
> the church on the reservation
> the witch-hangers and witchcraft
> the Bureau of Indian Affairs
> the coming of the Spanish
> the executive orders, the four
> ways to speak of your place
> > in it all

> There are ways to speak of
> the rape of children by gods

the court fines and red tape
the drunks and those who seek
the clan's sense of self
the seven governments
ways to speak of your place
         in it all

There are ways to speak of
the thirteen sacred societies
the sixteen clans of the mother line
the secular medical social orders
the long-ago coming of Estevanico
the long-ago coming of Coronado
ways to speak of your place
         in it all

There are ways to speak of
the deer hoof clankers and gourd rattles
the jerkey chango-knot and hoops
the tamarack willow pinon detilas ice caves
the cottonwood mesas holy water adobe
the snowbirds cranes woodrats chipmunks
ways to speak of your place
         in it all

It was sad, I tell you, sad, that the whole mournful, beautiful
song passed them by. They never heard a word of it. Only the
guitar and I were in tears by the time she finished.

Chapter 44
Ceremonials

U nexpectedly on the second night at Ole Cantina Peter Inkpen turned up to see the performance—so he said; but there was more motivation to his little visit than that. True, Santa Fe was nearby, but Peter's motives were never singular. He was all spruced up, even wore a rose in his lapel and smelled like a dandy. The three of us went for a walk.

The conversation was strained. We each kept attempting to speak at the same time and the moments of silence were awkward. He finally left, saying he had to drive back to Santa Fe that night because of a seven o'clock meeting the next morning.

After he left I told the Turtle not to be surprised if she and I both would have to look for a new agent before long. True, Peter was making money off Painted Turtle but surely not enough to keep him very interested in handling her.

Meanwhile, we moved on. She kept making up new songs and singing them in these places we kept going to. Of course we went back often to the regular ones—Ranchito's in Gallup, the Stardust in Phoenix, the Lazy L in Albuquerque, the Blackbird in Cuba. But it was fun when we were headed for a town we had never been to before; fun anticipating what it would be like and what would happen; how the people would turn out to be. We spent the whole summer that way: moving around.

She happened to have a long engagement at Ranchito's in August so we were in Gallup the whole month. If you know Gallup you know August was not the time to be there. Just walking on the sidewalk your shoes would fry like eggs on a grill. There was a desert stillness in the air that conjured up thirst every minute.

Then there was the parade. I didn't really want to see it. You know, it's just an event for tourists but we were stuck in the city so we went. There we were, sitting on the curb, with the anglos and the Mexicans, waiting to see Indians. I felt silly; the Turtle thought it was funny. As a child she had once or twice marched with the Olla Maidens, carrying one end of the Zuni banner, with another little girl who carried the other end.

We were early—having no place else to go. They would start down at Sixth and come up Sixty-six, as usual, then turn south into First, come over to Coal Avenue, then head west along Coal, back down Sixth. We were waiting near the corner of First and Coal. The police cars kept cruising by. Through a loudspeaker they warned owners of parked cars that their vehicles would be towed if not moved right away. Down at First they had the tow truck ready with the driver at the wheel. In about ten minutes all the cars and trucks were driven away except one. They brought the tow truck up and backed it up to the front of the lone car. Just as they were about to hook up the old car, an old Mexican came running up the street shaking his fist at them. When he got there he stopped shaking his fist and started grinning and apologizing. They let him drive away. The incident provided a little amusement for those of us waiting for the Indians.

We heard them before we saw them. They were a block over, headed this way. The first group was Hopi. I recognized only one old man: a boyhood friend of my grandfather's. I forget his name. The kids were carrying the Hopi banner in front of the paraders. Watching them—these were probably mainly people from Third Mesa—gave me the crawlies. Then a dance group called Aztec came. They were just professional entertainers, I think. Next came the Acoma people. Leading them was a famous Indian from Taos. Spectators stood and clapped and waved when he came along. He was in headgear and buckskin. A proud figure, he waved back to the crowd. Then he saw us and after getting over his surprise, strutted over to the Turtle and me and, without losing a step of rhythm, whispered, "This parade is like a waiting room in a hospital." And he broke into a gut-splitting laugh as he strutted away, regaining his lead. I watched the old Ceremonials hero till he was out of sight.

Now, the Zunis. Beside me, I felt Painted Turtle grow stiff. The two little girls came around the corner of First carrying the banner. I said, "Here you go." She closed her eyes for a moment and shook her head. After the banner-carriers were older girls in blue uniforms, twirling sticks and high-stepping; behind them, boys beat drums hung from their necks—others blew bugles. I glanced at the Turtle. She was scrutinizing the faces. A whole new Black Rock generation? The marchers' faces were swollen with pride or terror; I couldn't tell which. Then the Olla Maidens came. Oh, God. Spare me! They were wonderful, wonderful!—but unbendable as wood! But that was the point: discipline; and they carried the clay pots with great dignity. This, the Turtle told me in a whisper, was in no way a sacred dance. The Zunis shared it all the time with strangers. I had seen it before—without a great deal of interest. The Olla Maidens were in no way maidens. The average age must have been forty—if a day. The pots were, of course, on their heads. They were in traditional dress of sash and leggins and wore lots of jewelry. The Turtle told me, as they went by, that these same women had been doing this march since they were little girls. Some of them originally carried the banner or marched with the high school steppers. At the National Guard Armory they would perform their stiff rain dance and sing the "Buffalo Song" and the "Airplane Song" and when finished, walk stiffly out of the light. She said her grandfather used to say of the Ceremonials and the Zunis in it, "We march with pots on head. White sponsor makes money."

Well, the Turtle couldn't go to the rodeo at the Armory even if she had wanted to—and I certainly had no desire to go with her or alone. I had never gone that far out of my way to see Indians entertain the anglos and the Mexicans. The rodeo, as far as I knew, had always been a night affair. So when a Mexican came along after the parade trying to sell tickets to the rodeo we sent him on down the line.

Chapter 45
An Interlude: My Story

We were headed back to Bombay in early October—because they wanted her back—and it was, I think, a Monday night, and we were approaching the Antelope Mesa turn-off for the Hopi Villages when I got this bright idea that I wanted the Turtle to meet my folks—wanted them to meet her. It was a crazy, spur-of-the-moment impulse. I asked her how she felt about it. I wanted her to say some other time but she told me she felt all right about meeting Ruth and Mike. I said heck they probably are already turned in for the night. The lights hadn't been working too well lately. Power failure. She thought this a lame reason for not going, so we went.

I'd never told her very much about them or my past and she had never asked. Oh, maybe she knew some things about me. Having a Navajo father in Hopi land wasn't exactly a picnic. Hopis had had nothing but a history of trouble with them Navajos. My mom had trouble with my dad. So it goes.

They were still up although it was nine—their bedtime. They were polite and she was polite. Ruth insisted on feeding us. After dinner, the Turtle and I went outside and sat on the step. The October moon was a thing to behold. You know how it is.

She said she felt stuffed. We had had lamb stew and boiled midget corn and frybread. I felt good, less nervous.

I knew I was fishing for a response that night when I asked her what did she think. I didn't know exactly what I wanted her to respond to, but I wanted it. She laughed at my question. I laughed at my own confusion. We then hugged. She whispered, when I turned her free, in my ear: my parents, she said, were wonderful, good people—I should be proud of them. I blushed. She didn't see it, I'm sure. But somehow this reponse didn't satisfy me—I still felt, uh, I don't know, something lacking, wanting: a kind of terrible churning in my stomach, in my chest.

We sat there. The moon was with us. To my left, I saw the light come on and—in ten minutes—go out in my parent's bedroom. They were finished for the night. I looked up at the expanse of stars. I pointed to Third Mesa and told the Turtle what she already knew: them folks over there didn't have much to do with us over here. I couldn't think of anything else to say. Then she asked me, as she hugged my arm, what was it like growing up here, with the sky like this, out there over Keams Canyon. I didn't take the question as a signal. I was still feeling pretty down. Yet I tried. I told her I was bigger than the other kids my age and felt really self-conscious about it. It was the truth. Mike, I said, had owned some sheep when he was younger but later made most of his money from the rugs he wove. So I didn't have the usual sheep camp experience most reservation boys have. Most years Ruth made more money than Mike from the pots she made: pots sold better and faster; they were easier to make. I remembered helping her lug them to market. An agency sold her pots to shops throughout the Southwest. The Turtle and I that night discovered that my mother's pots and her grandmother's jewelry sold in some of the same shops in Arizona and New Mexico. I felt her kiss my ear. It felt good—made me laugh. I told her I look at the little kids around First Mesa and get reminded of myself when I was little—speaking Tusayan and broken English. It wasn't till I went away and came back, I said, that I saw this place with its dust and harshness and bad smells. When I joined the army and was sent to California I was shocked, I told her, by how big everything out there was. Corn was huge, people were my size or larger. In Hawaii, it was the same: giant-size fruit. I got back to Tewa and saw, for the first time, that my mother's people were really midgets. I was twenty before I stopped stooping just to be like everybody else. I learned to hold my head up like my father, like the Navajos. She asked me if I danced when I was little. I told her about the ceremonies I knew—the Sotaluna, the Snake-Dance, the Flute, the unmasked ones too—the Bean-Planting, the Antelope, the others. I was a good dancer and a lot of my self-consciousness was under control by the time I was fifteen as a result. I told her I liked the dances but was often a loner who used to go off alone walking down into the desert or away in the other direction. I liked lying on a secluded spot and gazing into Keams Canyon, dreaming of my future. Back then I wasn't planning on being a musician. I thought I'd win a scholarship and become a basketball star and retire rich at age twenty-five. I was certainly tall enough. And skinny enough. We laughed at this and she playfully punched me in the stomach. But I gave up the thought of basketball after one semester on the high-school team. It was so embarrassing I didn't even want to talk about it: I didn't make one single basket. Instead, my father taught me to help him weave and I learned something about making pots too. I told her about my uncle Joe Polacca, whose fraternity I joined as a boy, and how he taught me jewelry-making. She said she wished she had known me as a child. She wished that we had grown up together, maybe somewhere in another world. We kissed. Then we were silent for a long time. She gazed at a single star till tears formed in her eyes. She asked me then who had been my first girl. I laughed at my memory of her—Geraldine of the Green Corn Clan. What was she like? Her family lived in a filthy house, one which smelled like its slopjar and had only a dirt floor where the old women sat making pots to sell at market. Geraldine's father was very, very old and the people at Walpi, high on the cliff there, where she lived, doubted that he could have been the real father. That was the joke about Geraldine and her family. The old man had a pockmarked face.

A cloud moved in front of the moon. The sky was kidney-colored. We sat there in silence and I thought about being kidded for being a half-breed, all the years—since early childhood—of enduring that kidding. There was a lot of anger in me because of it. People up here thought the Navajos pretty loose and arrogant and without traditions. A high-school teacher once told the class that the Navajos were nomad bums. Everybody looked at me. I knew the Zunis had strict and severe beliefs about half-breeds but I also knew that Painted Turtle was not prejudiced. Still, I didn't want to get angry that night—and I would have had I started talking about how it had been growing up half Navajo among Hopis, who, after all, live on a postage stamp-size piece of land smack in the middle of the Navajo reservation—which is the largest one, as far as I know, anywhere. But my father told me things that made the Navajos sound like heroes to me. I had to keep these victorious stories to myself on the playground during sessions of bravado. The other boys would simply have laughed at me had I told them my great-grandfather went to Washington with an Indian expedition on three separate occasions to protest unfair reservation conditions imposed by law. The cloud slowly moved across the moon as I thought of my father telling me this and the other stories—about the Navajo fight against tuberculosis and venereal disease—he used to tell. No, it was better to keep everything simple, even a little funny, at least warm and friendly. If she wants to hear more, I thought, tell her about the time I had to decide between joining my father's fraternity or my uncle's. Big decision. It almost broke me. But now it seemed funny. I suddenly laughed, thinking about it.

Painted Turtle said, What? and I told her about the time. There was the rivalry between my mother's brother and my father. The one I decided to go with would have to weave a special ceremonial kilt and sash for me. My father had been looking forward to doing this for a year or more. He was very disappointed when I decided to join Uncle Joe's lodge. I told the Turtle I wished now I hadn't; but then—I'm ashamed to say—I knew my father was looked upon with suspicion in his own lodge merely because of his Navajo background and I wanted no part of joining him as a target. I figured I'd suffered enough already. It hurt him badly, I said, and I still feel the pain hurting him caused me.

She said she wanted to walk a bit. The bright moon was again unobstructed and lighted the path we took away from the village. It had been on this same path, I told her, that I went forth on my first jackrabbit hunt. Rather than coming back empty-handed me and the two other boys pooled our coins and bought a couple of rabbits at the trading post. Our trick was discovered, I said, and we caught hell. The rabbits were supposed to be for a ceremonial occasion and the fact that we had lied about how we got them was thought a bad, bad sign. Telling the Turtle now in moonlight was a kind of purging. I wasn't proud of the incident but for the first time in my life I felt I could share the bad things of my life as well as the good without being judged too harshly.

The darkness helped, though. If I was unwinding, confessing, giving her more of myself, I needed this moon-lit darkness—not because I feared her; rather, because I feared myself. The jackrabbit trick, like the joining of my uncle's kiva rather than my father's, hurt my father. Seems I was always hurting Mike. I couldn't help it—or, I thought I couldn't help it. I told the Turtle how I had refused to go to his kiva with him to talk with the old men who'd initiated Mike years before at their Nahtna. It didn't seem important, then, and I wasn't about to put myself out. Damnit, I said, I was pretty selfish! She agreed. When she agreed I fell silent.

We walked on. I asked her, finally, if her agreement meant she loved me less. She said no—that it had nothing to do with that. It was just an opinion.

After I was silent for awhile, the Turtle began to talk. She told me she thought my mother had modern ideas. She said she envied me for my mother. Modern ideas? Ruth? I couldn't believe what I was hearing. She said, Yes, modern. I wanted her to say why. Well, she said, at dinner Ruth had talked about her political work in the community. She never once mentioned the church. I saw my mother, the size of a normal ten-year-old child, sitting there at the table, her feet barely touching the floor. Modern? In all of my thirty-three years I never thought of my mother as modern! Painted Turtle said she thought they were good together. Something else I never gave a thought! So, Mike went off to play cards with the guys in his kiva; when Ruth was tired of pot-making, she played bingo with the women at the church's rec center. She took my hand and swung my arm. Another thing: the television. What about it? Well, she said, they don't just watch it stupidly. They select certain programs to watch. Before dinner, she reminded me, Ruth and Mike had checked the newspaper for the TV listing and having found nothing of interest had decided against turning it on after dinner.

Okay, that was all true. But my mother, I told the Turtle, still called the village Tiwan or Tiweash and wrote the word as T-e-b-a-s. Nothing modern about that! I told her how much Ruth loved her father—Acacofui—who insisted till his dying day that the proper name was Chiguas. I told her how bewildering the old man had been for me and how, at twelve, because I had on one occasion not shown proper respect for him—a descendant of one of the oldest families east of the Rio Grande—I was dismissed as hopeless.

We stopped. We could see from where we stood the Antelope Mesa. We had entered the Hopi-land there. She recognized it, even in moonlight. She said, "That's the road we came up."

Chapter 46
A Song Itself

I wanted to cry but could only make a mental sign of the deer-bone crisscrossed in an attempt to soothe the carpentry of my spine. This was the way I reacted to the song she made up for me that night at First Mesa.

> Your blood comes up
> from sixteen million acres
> of worthless land
> You are my nomad
> pray to the kachinas
> Wave your blanket at me
> I'll be your smoke signals
> Be a movie Indian
> I'll be your audience
> I'll eat your mutton
> sleep through your tb
> suffer your vd
> Your blood comes up
> through sixty-two thousand
> strong in this harsh desert
> Dress me in your sheepskin
> share my Coca-Cola
> love me in your log-hut
> I make you blood
> of my blood

I was at once so moved and exposed that I felt—I don't know exactly how I felt; I do know I had not felt as helpless since going with great uncertainty into the ceremony of my initiation after the rabbit hunt, with my jeans down, and feeling my uncle stick the rabbit's nose between the cheeks of my butt. I learned my faith in Old Acacofui's One Horn Society. I also learned to not take it so seriously. But that was another story.

Painted Turtle and I drove away from Tewa the next morning into a glorious sunrise. I don't believe I ever felt greater happiness in my whole life. My spirit was sleeping comfortably in sunken deltas of bighorn old as time; I was as joined together as tree and earth. Where before in my spirit bobcats had sung like jays and muledeer acted like mice and black-tailed hares barked like chipmunks, now love turned me into the flesh of a song itself. I can't describe it.

The sun came all the way up and moved to the center of the sky. We kept driving till it went down on the other side. In the middle the day was hot then cooler. I think I understood the woman next to me and how death and life and time—everything!—went into and came out of that Sacred Lake we had searched for—and, in our own way, found. In this state of mind I came as close as I possibly could to accepting what we had there between us and to also accepting the fact of our different ways and death and the old people, too, and their ways.

> When somebody dies
> they turn the mirror
> around before they
> bring him in
> for the washing

Chapter 47
The Hunt

Old Leekela had come into the graveyard while they—they said—were digging the grave for Mrs. Vera Hamilton, a famous silversmith (as though they'd needed to remind her who Mrs. Hamilton was!) and Old Leekela told them he was their grandpa. Painted Turtle stamped her foot on the ground and bit her lip to keep from cursing. This was, oh, about a month ago, back when it was still summer. Maybe two months ago.

She was sitting on the front steps with them. I was in Gallup waiting for her to come back. The twins told her about going on the rabbit hunt with Old Leekela. The nerve of that old man to approach her sons! She wanted to know what he said to them. She had never told them about their father—about the rape. Both boys, physically larger than she now, fed the narrative like two cowpokes trying to rope the same calf. They finished Mrs. Hamilton's grave and the boy from the councilman brought them two dollars each, then they went with Old Leekela out toward Corn Mountain. Like Grandpa Waldo—who was ill in bed with an unknown condition—Old Leekela carried a bottle in his back pocket. As they walked behind him on the narrow path they saw him nip from it occasionally.

She cringed as she listened. Old Leekela had with him his bow and sachel of arrows on his back. Like the old man, they kicked at bushes or whacked them with sticks, expecting rabbits to leap out. One finally did and Old Leekela missed. They scared up two or three others but each time Leekela missed. He kept nipping from his bottle. Then he let Bruce hold the bow and walked on out farther toward Corn Mountain. Then what happened? They said they kept kicking bushes. They came finally to and hit another bush with a jackrabbit hiding in it and it jumped out. It took off across the field and got some distance before Bruce could get the arrow into the bow. Bryce said he threw a stone at it and hit it but the stone didn't stop the jackrabbit.

The Turtle wanted know what Old Leekela talked about. They told her he talked about his son who had gone far away; where, nobody knows. He said he missed his son. What else? Old Leekela told them, they said, that his lost son was their father. Did they believe this? They both shrugged as though it meant very little whether or not they believed the story. They then told her they thought their father dead. Why, she wanted to know. Because they thought so, that's why. After a moment she said, "You have only me—and the family."

Chapter 48
Hard Ground

She sat by the body. She had gotten here in time this time. The remains of Waldo, bloated and naked, lay on the bed where all these years he had slept with her mother, where the Turtle first saw dimly in the night the lifting and falling of their lovemaking and from where for years while growing up she had heard their separate breathing and the difficulty of it. She sat there helping with the washing of her father's body, using a cotton cloth wet with warm water and yucca soap. Nobody had touched his penis yet. The women and the men of the clan worked up and down the legs and arms. Finally it became clear to Painted Turtle that she—as the closest one to it—would have to take up the penis of her father and prepare it along with the rest of him for the journey. She made the decision, then picked it up and began scrubbing it. There was no fear in her, and it was only slightly hard from death as she worked up and down and under it. She then cleaned his testicles with the same care. None of the others spoke or looked at her while she worked this area of the body.

They turned him over. The Turtle washed his buttocks and Marelda scrubbed the back. His mother Moira Crow Dog washed the left arm and his brother the right. When the Turtle finished with his bottom she moved down to the feet and, one at a time, scrubbed them as clean as they would come. The soles were hard

155

and crusty. The toenails were stubby and uneven.

The Turtle and the rest of them worked at him with silent respect and with a profound devotion to duty. The purification went on a long time. The relatives in the room who were not working at Waldo's body stood in quiet and patient stillness, waiting for the hour in which they all could begin to sew him into the last blanket he would wear in this earthly world.

The hole on the south side of the yard had already been dug. The twins had helped with the digging. His brother and a couple of cousins took him out and put him in the back of his own pickup. One drove the short distance over to the yard. The Turtle and the others walked over. There was not much to say. Without ceremony, they lowered him into place in the proper manner with his head in the right direction. Then the men took up the shovels and began to return the dirt, which before long covered the last visible inch of the bright red and green blanket with leaping deer and hunters with bow-and-arrows sprinting over bushes after them.

The Zuni Beautification Team had moved the old car so there was no place to sit alone with the boys so she sat down on the riverbank where she once sat with Old Larry Gchachu. Bryce sat on her left and Bruce on her right. The ground was hard and dry with the beginning of fall in the air. From a nearby house the sound of a storyteller on KSHI was telling a story in Zuni. She couldn't hear the words and no meaning—at this distance—was possible but she knew anyway what it was all about. The story was always the same. She hugged the boys to her then quickly released them with the gesture of a mother who wants to maintain a firm relationship with her children. Bruce finally spoke first. He said Grandpa was talking inside the blanket down in the ground.

Bryce said it wasn't so because dead people don't talk. Bruce said kachinas were dead people and they talked all the time. Bryce told Bruce he didn't know anything, that he was stupid. The Turtle told them both to stop it, not to fight. Back at the house the Turtle heard somebody call out to her, calling her Mary. Before she turned she knew it was Felix and that Lupe had finished cooking dinner and that it was time now for the whole family to sit down together and break bread and dip it into the stew and eat silently together out of respect for her dead father.

Epilogue

A week after Painted Turtle's father died I sold my Electra to Charles A. Dragoslav, owner of Cholly's Loans, Inc., down on Sixty-six and bought the pearl-inlaid Epiphone Deluxe that had hung on the wall there for something like five years. The death and my switching to manual weren't exactly related but I remembered them that way. The Turtle came back from her mourning with the family and we slowly resumed the life we had come to know together. The Bug was still running well and we were too so we packed our guitars in and got started.

We figured Peter probably wouldn't like the idea of us teaming up together as a duet but we were going to do it anyway. Since we were headed for the Blackbird in Cuba we figured that was as good a place as any to make our debut. We had had a few days to practice. Although it was getting cold, we would drive up in the mountains outside of Gallup, right after she got back from Zuni, and rehearse. I thought we sounded pretty good together but it was hard to tell out there in the open. The few times we tried rehearsing in the motel room people complained to the desk clerk and of course he came knocking on our door. But now we were on the road and feeling pretty confident that we had not only a love relationship we liked and wanted to keep but a musical one that was probably going to work equally well. Like I said before, I